WHAT'S COOKING GOOD LOOKING

Imagined and assembled by

Ashley Russell

May your copy of this book be written in
and loved like Nana's recipe cards —
stained with vanilla extract and
baking cocoa.

And sugar.

Recipes and family photos in this book were originally collected by Wanda, with additional sourcing from her family.

Cover photos: Wanda Sell on her honeymoon (with Bob) in 1959; Wanda and her sister Wynona Chastain.

FOOD PHOTOGRAPHY
Ashley Russell copyright © 2025

EDITOR
Vanessa Salvia

ILLUSTRATIONS
Abigail Agersea of SADPUPPY Tattoo copyright © 2025

RISOGRAPH PRINTS
Outlet PDX

PRINTED BY
Brown Printing Inc

ISBN
979-8-218-64953-1

2ND PRINTING 1ST EDITION

whatscookinggoodlookingrecipes.com
whatscookinggoodlookingrecipes@gmail.com
@whatscookinggoodlookingrecipes

Written by a real human bean.

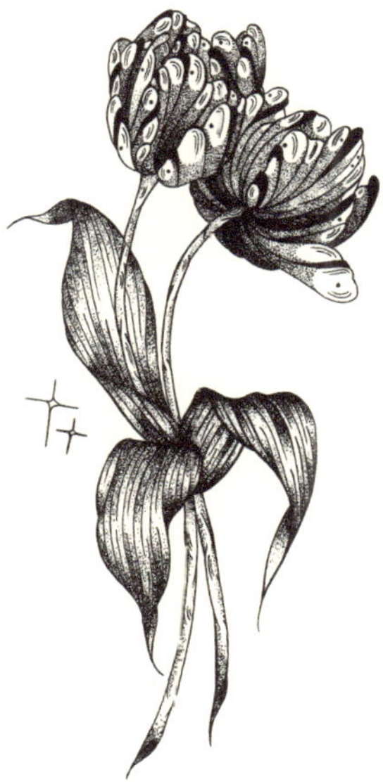

Wanda loved to cook for her family.
This recipe book is dedicated to all of her loved ones,
past, present, and future.

CONTENTS

135 NOW WE'RE COOKING

185 BLESS HER PEA-PICKIN' HEART

201 TO WET YOUR WHISTLE

215 FOR PETE'S SAKE

227 LEFTOVERS

-

253 INDEX

WANDA MAE SELL
1933-2024

SET THE SCENE

W.M.S.

Wanda Mae was born November 18, 1933, on the Inmon family farm in Corsicana, Texas, to Loyf David and Leona, also known as Memaw and Pawpaw. She was the youngest of eight children, four boys and four girls, closer in age to her two nieces than her siblings. Raised in a Church of Christ household, Wanda upheld her faith throughout her entire life. Married in her late adolescence, she became Mrs. Wanda Vaughn. Just about a year and a half after graduating high school, Wanda was gifted her first child, Angela Leona, in December of 1952. Shortly thereafter, Wanda separated from Angie's father and was looking for a fresh start. She and her daughter moved to Southern California with two of her newlywed friends from high school. Wanda began work at the Hacienda Motor Hotel, a resort destination off the coast of the Pacific Ocean in San Pedro. It is here that she met Robert Dean Sell from Nebraska. After falling deeply in love (and kissing in some bushes), Bob and Wanda were married on March 27, 1959. America's cultural decade kicked off with Wanda giving birth to Alicia Dean in April 1960, Robert Dean Jr. in July 1962, and Cynthia Marie in September 1969. Bob and Wanda raised their four children throughout the United States while Bob worked for GTE, a telephone operations company that published phone directories. He made his life work as a Director of Sales after being initially scouted as an artist for their phonebook print ads. Wanda was a devoted cook for her family and many GTE gatherings. She loved interior decorating and creating inviting table settings. During Bob and Wanda's life together, they lived in Southern California, Texas, Pennsylvania, Florida, New York, Hawaii, and Washington, doubling back to a handful of these states over the decades, eventually retiring in La Conner, Washington. The recipes in this book are a fitting homage to the diverse range of places the Sell family has lived. Angela's firstborn affectionately nicknamed Bob and Wanda "Nana" and "Pops," and it stuck like a wet noodle. Pops passed away in 2011; they were married for fifty-two years. As of 2024, Nana (pronounced Na-NAW in true Southern fashion) outlived her siblings. She is survived by her four children, five grandchildren, and one great-grandchild.

Ashley and Nana on Chuckanut Drive, Washington's original scenic byway, overlooking the Samish Bay. Mid to late 1990s.

INTRODUCTION

Wanda's meals, our family's holiday gatherings, the sharing of cooking secrets, and the food our parents provided have all been essential traditions and forms of nourishment. This book is a way to cherish time and remember these loving moments of breaking bread.

Thumbing through these pages is like listening to a mixtape of your favorite songs. Perhaps you may discover new perspectives, insights, or remixes of the classics. The collection spans a wide range, although it is heavy on the holiday dishes and sweet tooth cravings. One of my favorite parts of the book is the accessibility of the recipes. If you only have a few ingredients in your pantry, are a new cook, or own a limited number of kitchen supplies, there are recipes for you. If a certain type of meat is on sale where you like to shop, or you are on a budget with your family, you have meal options.

I included this introduction because I am not 100% confident that the recipes and chapter introductions convey the essence of Bob, Wanda, and the Sell family. I want to share the nuances, family stories, favorite memories, and the sensations they evoke. I want to share what I learned while creating this book. What I will always miss and what I want to carry on. I hope this book gives you a sense of who my grandma was as a person, as told by me.

"When someone is offering you food, they're telling you a story. They are telling you about themselves; where they come from, who they are, what makes them happy." – *Anthony Bourdain*

This book is a love letter. It's a love letter to my grandparents, my mom, and my whole family. I can only imagine what it's like to be a Kennedy, a Soprano, a Presley, or even a Windsor, but it feels like I have my version of this in the Sells. Growing up, I would hear stories about my grandparents, my mom, and her siblings – it felt like they were famous. They each did incredible, hilarious, only "in a certain time and place" things that subconsciously and inherently made me, me.

I am a grandchild, so I did not experience Bob and Wanda the same way as their children. Everyone knows that grandchildren get a much different version of their parents' parents than they did. My intention and hope is that anyone from my family reading this will see their own experiences, memories, and feelings in mine. I hope this love story to my family inspires you and your family, just as great love stories often do.

I was born in 1988. I moved all the drinks out of the way to find the Sunny D in the fridge. I had dial-up internet and religiously used AOL Instant Messenger. I loved the Spice Girls. I was on the school bus to seventh grade on the morning of September 11th. I had my first cell phone, a Nokia brick, as a senior in high school. I can turn a document into a PDF and re-wind a cassette tape with a pencil. I was alive during the tragedy of JonBenét, the saga of the O.J. Simpson trial, the loss of Kurt Cobain and Princess Diana, the drama of Monica Lewinsky, the Mary Kay Letourneau scandal, Y2K, and the breakup of Justin and Britney (#FreeBritney). I believe in mental health, self-care, people before profit, and the climate clock. I believe in equality, freedom of choice, and not being a judgmental a-hole. I believe that learning how to follow your heart can take decades. I believe that healing your heart can take just as long.

Wanda, whether you called her Mom, Nana, Nanaw, Mrs. Sell, Miss Wanda, Ommie, or The Gum Lady, had such a one-of-a-kind Southern accent. One that, for a long time, was just how "grandmas" talked in my mind. She had a very specific way of putting on lipstick; maybe one day it will go viral. She held her hands a certain way, shaped her nails a certain way. She had a specific fragrance, Amarige by Givenchy, for those interested. Strawberries and sugar cooking on the stovetop smell like Nana...iced tea and lemons smell like Nana...cornbread dressing cooking in the oven smells like Nana. She washed dishes in the hottest water imaginable. Her hugs, her laugh, her smile. The way a smile would slowly come onto her face. The way she sang me songs goodnight. I can hear her singing. When she woke up in the morning, she would hold the bed sheet over her mouth because of morning breath – how polite. Her obsession with *The Young & The Restless* and the QVC channel. She hated snakes. She didn't like avocados or salmon. Or slow drivers. She would pour vinegar on my hair after she took me to the pool. The way she decorated her house. Her handwriting. When she got really into learning calligraphy, I loved those special pens. She loved animals. Dr Pepper. Swedish Fish. Doublemint gum.

She put her fries on her burgers. She wore giant sunglasses over her already giant eyeglasses. The way she would "try on" clothes in the department store by holding up the garment's side seams and inseams to her proportions. She had these deep, loving hazel-green eyes. She loved flowers; she always knew their names. She'd always make me lemon squares; they were my favorite. She loved card games. She loved crocheting baby blankets. She sewed throughout her life, making clothes for all of us from time to time. I still have the baby clothes she made for me, and the Dorothy dress she made for me one Halloween. She awakened a love of sewing in me. Over the summers, she would take me to the local library so I could participate in reading contests and check out dozens of books. Driving to their house, the famous red bridge over the Swinomish Channel in La Conner will always be "Nana's bridge." She was calm, warm, and comforting, but also a firecracker. While making this cookbook, my Aunt Angie mentioned that I am half my mom and half Nana. Not knowing my Dad, this observation helped bring peace to the ever-dormant wonder about the other half of my gene pool. I see a great deal of both Wanda and my Mom in me, and that's more than enough familial backstory for a strong sense of self.

Bob, Robert, Bobby, Dad, Pops was magnetic, larger than life. He would laugh at that because of his giant belly. His laugh – I can hear it. I can hear him yelling "Wanda!" in the house. I know we all can. He thought he was the funniest of them all. That makes me chuckle. His jolly demeanor. His humor. His short fuse. His endless helping hand. He loved to talk on the phone. He would often make prank phone calls to us. He made everyone feel at home. He was my mom's best friend. He was my uncle's best friend. He would stand on the front porch and wave bye-bye as we drove out of their driveway. He frequently watched the stock market. He wore matching velour sweat suits with Crocs. Fashion. Icon. He had a particular scent, Polo Eau De Toilette, for those interested. It filled the house, the car, your nostrils, and your memory. You look at a picture of him and can smell him. He loved a good deal. He could always be found at secondhand stores, buying golf clubs. His car(s) should have had the bumper sticker "Will Brake for Garage Sales." He would scare me and my cousins late at night by coming up to the windows outside their La Conner home, which was surrounded by dark woods, wearing vintage Halloween masks he found at yard sales. How very David Lynch of him. He would take Nana and me to the buffet and have the restaurant staff announce over the loudspeaker, "Bob Sell's granddaughter Ashley Russell is visiting him from Seattle." He would take me to the pool and let me surf on his back. A famous family story now: he asked me for a kiss and I paused and said, "I'll high five ya." He thought that was hilarious. He always tried to cheat at Scrabble and Skip-Bo. He loved animals and always kept horses. He would order cutting-edge gadgets from infomercials and ask me to assemble them. He would tell his grandkids to run uphill for nickels or pull weeds for pennies. We always suspected we were getting the short end of the deal. We all thought he was someone who would live forever and always be there, this massive presence in all of our lives.

Bob and Wanda loved to dance. They lit up when they danced. Pops would dance with me. They were so playful; they set that tone, that vibe. Pops loved to tease Nana. That mischievousness is alive in all of us. If there could have been tabloids about my grandparents and their kids, there would have been. Now that I am a little older, I see this Inmon/Sell spark in my cousins and me.

Some of my favorite stories...Pops putting the car in cruise control and "resting his eyes" while my mom, several years shy of a license, steered the vehicle. My mom, maybe 13, wanted a bikini and hoop earrings, and when Wanda said no way, she washed cars with her friend and bought them herself, running through the house in her itsy bitsy bikini, proud. Cindy put FOR SALE signs all over her high school's front yard and fell into the boys' locker room while peeking in from the ceiling tiles. An old wives' tale claims that Angie was so short she had to sit on phone books while driving her VW bug. On a cross-country road trip, two cars were full of the family. They stopped at a gas station, and each car thought the other had Bob Jr. in it when they caravanned away. Arriving at their destination, they realized no one had Bob Jr., so they had to frantically drive back to retrieve him. Pops sold his radio to buy a wedding cake for his and Wanda's special day. Wanda went into a rushing river after a young Bob Jr. fell in and waited there, digging her feet in the mud and holding onto him until Bob showed up on a horse to save them both. Pops drove horses from California to Washington on one of their cross-country moves and let them run on the beach off Highway 101 (I'm envisioning a Brad Pitt blockbuster here). My mom goes in to buy worms for a fishing trip, and the clerk tells her they only have night crawlers. She asks if they work during the day. Pops puts a picture of Nana in the front bathroom because she didn't like any paintings he would try to put there. Hilarious. All the stories of my mom sticking up for Bob Jr. as kids. The story of my mom's bunny passing away, so Nana and Pops replaced it with a completely different bunny. When she came home from school, she saw the bunny, shrugged, and continued with her afternoon. She thought it was like the horse of a different color from the Wizard of Oz. These stories go on and on, and I never get tired of hearing them.

My family is, and never has been, picture perfect — not while I've been in it, and from what I've heard, not before I was born. It feels like this needs to be said, not to take away from, but to add to this story. During the conflicts and broken hearts we have endured at each other's hands, I know we can and do celebrate all the love and laughter our family shares with each other. Nothing is black and white. Everything is grey. Or rainbow. Rainbow is better. More colorful, more accurate. What is a great love story without a bit of tragedy, a tornado, a rainbow after a storm, anyway?

I learned a great deal while creating this book. I learned that dark-colored baking pans absorb and distribute heat faster than lighter-colored pans, resulting in quicker baking. I learned that oleo is a type of margarine and that salad oil is a type of vegetable oil. That "Sheath Cake" may just be a regional mispronunciation of Texas Sheet Cake. Pecan trees are native to the Southeast United States, and this is likely why Wanda put pecans in almost every baked good. That sweet milk is a Southern term that refers to fresh, whole milk, as a distinction from buttermilk. My favorite new baking hack: if you don't have buttermilk, you can put fresh lemon juice in milk and make your own buttermilk. I learned that heating measuring cups and spoons under hot water makes it easier to scoop out peanut butter and shortening. I learned that women's groups throughout the decades were known for creating spiral-bound cookbooks. That Betty Crocker wasn't a real person. I am still learning that grocery shopping and dishes are a part of cooking. I learned how to format recipes, make dinner every night of the week outside of a pandemic, and how food brings people joy. I was reminded that food is not just medicine. It's not just to be watched, avoided, or a burden to make. That food is pleasure, it's a memory. And that's precisely what all the recipes in this book are.

I learned how much I love my family. I learned how much my family loves each other. I was constantly reminded about how much Bob and Wanda mean to us. I was touched by how much Bob and Wanda loved each other. I learned how to be vulnerable and ask for help and support. The process of making this book brought our family closer together. It gave us a reason to stay in touch when we maybe couldn't come up with one – trying to figure out who's who in old photos, deciphering what a recipe card says, sharing favorite memories and meals, reading drafts, and making suggestions. This connection with my family is something I know I needed and am most thankful for. Nana passed away in June 2024. Not too long after, my Aunt Cindy lost her fluffy golden retriever lab mix, Bahama, the sweetest, underwear-eating girl you'll ever meet. My mom and I lost Blondie, the coolest, most punk-rock pup, at the long and too-soon age of seventeen. She was my little sister. My cousin Kaelin, just months after marrying her high school sweetheart, unexpectedly lost her mother-in-law, Kim. I hope reading this book and enjoying its recipes can help bring a little comfort, in whatever way you need it.

Nana saw me for me. She always encouraged me to be a writer. She knew that I always see the good in the people I love, even when they may not be the best for me. She told me I was a good person. "Such a neat girl." Bracing myself for how she would feel about my tattoos over the years, one day she looked at me and said, "you really like these," with a slight smile. There can be such a stigma around mental health, and she remarked frankly on my melancholy as a young adult, wanting to know if I was okay. Who knows what else she knew about me that I was too naive, guarded to notice. She didn't let her own reflection get in the way, even with her personal, generational, and spiritual beliefs. It's only now that I realize what a gift that was. I wish I could have appreciated this when I had the chance to bond with her, confide in her, and learn from her. Instinctively, I felt it. Unconditional love is likely the best definition. I always felt safe. I hope Nana had someone who saw her. I hope we each come across at least one, hopefully many, of these types of connections in our lives and are awake enough to notice and return the kindness. Perhaps over a shared meal.

Upon further contemplation, the timing of making this book was inescapable; the writing bubbled out of me, and I devoured the entire process. Given all that had happened over the past year, over a lifetime, I was searching for a way to honor lost love, celebrate it, and find healing. Hungry for what my next chapter would be. Searching for a way to balance nourishment and movement. Not be overworked, but not be underworked. Balance consuming and creating. Even tilt the scales towards creating. In writing this book, I discovered that cooking is a perfect practice in this yin-yang balance. Researching how dishes are prepared, decoding ancient cursive, and sharing homemade meals have helped me re-find, re-balance, and re-ground myself.

If Gen X was the lost generation in the kitchen, what does that make us millennials? Or Gen Z? Or the generations after us? Feels like we have to start from scratch. But really, we have to find what was there all along. There's no place like home, after all.

Wanda outside her La Conner home in the early 1990s.

NANA'S PANTRY

A list of ingredients and supplies used time and time again in Wanda's recipes.

INGREDIENTS

- All-purpose flour
- Almond extract
- Bacon grease
- Baking chocolate
- Baking cocoa
- Baking powder
- Baking soda
- Black tea
- Butter and margarine
- Canned pumpkin
- Chocolate morsels
- Condensed milk
- Corn syrup
- Cream cheese
- Cream of tartar
- Cabbage
- Eggs
- Evaporated milk
- Garlic cloves
- Graham crackers
- Granulated sugar
- Jell-O packs
- Lemons
- Lots of love
- Mini marshmallows
- Onions
- Peanuts
- Peanut butter
- Pecans
- Powdered sugar
- Pudding mixes
- Red food coloring
- Salt and black pepper
- Spices
- Shortening
- Tomatoes
- Vanilla extract
- Vegetable oil
- White and yellow cake mix
- White chocolate almond bark
- Yellow and red potatoes

SUPPLIES

- Aluminum foil
- Baking dishes: glass, stainless steel
- Blender
- Butter knife
- Fluted tube pan
- Can opener
- Cake and pie pans
- Cake/pie server
- Cake stand with lid
- Candy thermometer
- Cast iron pan
- Cooling racks
- Cupcake liners
- Cutting knives
- Double boiler
- Food processor
- Food storage containers with lids
- Hand or stand mixer
- Kitchen towels
- Loaf and sheet pans
- Measuring utensils
- Meat thermometer
- Microwave
- Mixing bowls
- Parchment paper
- Plastic wrap
- Pot holders
- Resealable zip-top bags
- Rolling pin
- Spatula
- Sifter
- Slow cooker
- Stainless steel pots and pans
- Stockpot
- Toothpicks
- Whisk
- Wooden spoon

"Wanda, you've outdone yourself again!"

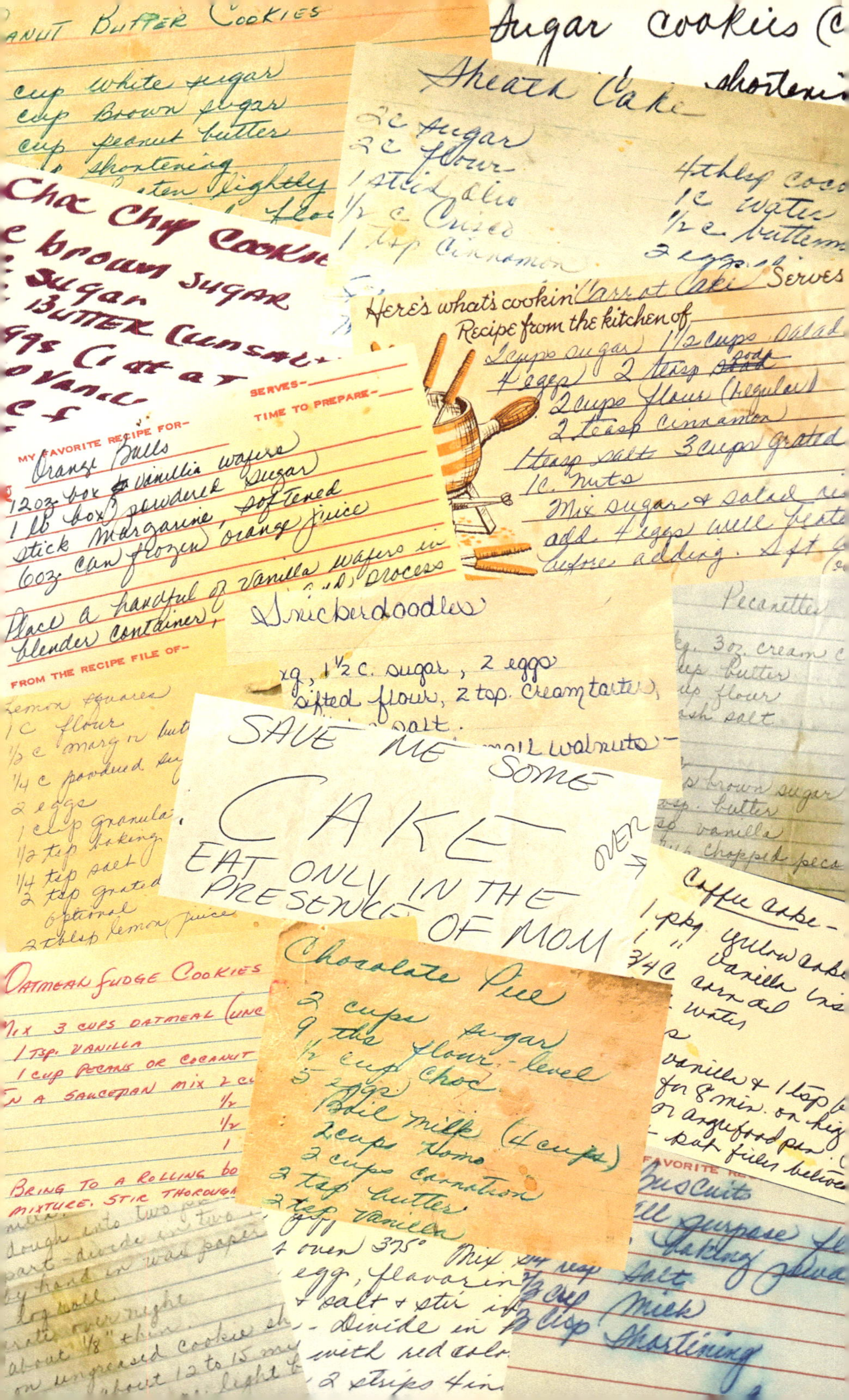

Sugar cookies
Sheath Cake
Carrot Cake
Here's what's cookin'
Recipe from the kitchen of
Chock Chip Cookies
MY FAVORITE RECIPE FOR-
Orange Balls
FROM THE RECIPE FILE OF-
Snickerdoodles
Pecanettes
Lemon Squares
SAVE ME SOME CAKE
EAT ONLY IN THE PRESENCE OF MOM
OVER
Coffee cake
Oatmeal Fudge Cookies
Chocolate Pie
Biscuits

Pound Cake
1/4 tsp. soda
3 cup sugar
3 cup flour
1 cup Crisco
1 cup buttermilk
Pecan Pie
1 cup pecans
1 cup dark Karo
2 T. flour
1 T. butter
2 eggs beaten
3/4 to 1 cup sugar
1 tsp Vanilla
Mix together & pour
Cornbread Dressing
PREPARATION TIME
NUMBER OF SERVINGS
SOURCE OF RECIPE
Crumble cornbread
6 slices bread broken up
set aside
onion
celery
saute til
SERVES-
TIME TO PREP.
FAVORITE RECIPE FOR-
CRUST
SHORT. LESS 1 TBLSP
BOILING WATER
FORK TIL SMOOTH. SIFT 1
1/2 TSP SALT STIR QUICKLY
BETWEEN TWO PIECES WAX PAPER
RECIPE FILE OF- WANDA
Here's what's cookin' Rice Patties
Recipe from the kitchen of Grandma
Corn Bread
Favorite Recipe
Bake 400° til firm
Here's what's cookin' Divinity Candy
Recipe from the kitchen of
1 c. sugar
1/2 c. water
1/2 cup white syrup
Cook until hard boil
beat whites of 2 eggs
stiff. Add slowly
syrup & add 1 tsp
& beat til gloss
from candy. Drop by
Chocolate Fudge
cups granulated sugar
can condensed milk
sticks butter
tsp. Vanilla
Marshmallows 10oz pkg
pkg Chocolate Chips
(3cups) pound pecans
Pour into large buttered pan.
Beat egg
+ cream of tartar
Stand in
Add 3/4 cup
coffee
Add one cup
beaten
Wanda
Before I forget it I'm sending you
Watergate Salad Recipe
1 cup nut
1 box pistachio instant pudding
1 box (9 oz) cool whip
1 large can crushed pineapple
1 pk. Small Marshmellows
Fudge - Top Secret -
cube butter
12 oz pkg choc chips
tsp Vanilla
eggs (whole)
powdered sugar

"Old age, I decided, is a gift. I am now, probably for the first time in my life, the person I have always wanted to be...

Whose business is it if I choose to read until 4:00 a.m. and sleep until noon? I will dance with myself to those wonderful tunes of the 1950s & 1960s, and if I, at the same time, wish to weep over a lost love, I will...

Sure, over the years, my heart has been broken. How can your heart not break when you lose a loved one...Broken hearts are what give us strength and understanding and compassion...

I am so blessed to have lived long enough to have my hair turn gray and to have my youthful laughs be forever etched into deep grooves on my face...

As you get older, it is easier to be positive. You care less about what other people think. I don't question myself anymore. I've even earned the right to be wrong.

So, to answer your question, I like being old. It has set me free. I like the person I have become.

I am not going to live forever, but while I am still here, I will not waste time lamenting what could have been or worrying about what will be. And I shall eat dessert every single day (if I feel like it)."

- *Author Unknown*

Wanda reposted this on her social media account in 2011 after the loss of Pops.

Versions of this quote have been attributed to the likes of Ed Saltzman and Judi Dench, but most versions have been reposted numerous times with no clear connection to the original author...

No matter, the message resonates with who Wanda was to all of us and is a great way to kick off her recipes: make it sweet!

LIFE
IS
WHAT
YOU
BAKE IT

BANANA BREAD

METHOD

1. Preheat oven to 325 degrees. Set aside 2 greased and floured regular-size loaf pans or 4 mini loaf pans.
2. In a large bowl, beat together sugar and shortening until well combined.
3. Add eggs until smooth and creamy. Add vanilla. Set aside.
4. In a small bowl, combine baking soda and buttermilk; add alternately with flour to the large bowl mixture.
5. Mix in bananas. Stir in nuts, if desired.
6. Pour into prepared loaf pans, filling 1/2 to 3/4 full.
7. It will take 1 hour to 1 hour 15 minutes to bake 1 regular loaf pan or 2 mini loaf pans in the preheated oven. Insert a toothpick or a butter knife into the center; if it comes out mostly clean (with just a few crumbs, if any), the bread is done.
8. Let cool for about 10 minutes before removing it from the loaf pan and placing it on a cooling rack.
9. Let banana bread sit unwrapped overnight for that ultimate sticky top texture.
10. Serve in slices.
11. To store, wrap banana bread tightly in plastic wrap or foil, or place it in an airtight container. Keep at room temperature.

INGREDIENTS

- 3 cups granulated sugar
- 1 cup shortening
- 4 eggs
- 2 teaspoons vanilla extract
- 2 teaspoons baking soda
- 1 and 1/2 cups buttermilk
- 4 cups sifted all-purpose flour
- 5 large well-bruised bananas, peeled and mashed
- 1 cup chopped nuts, optional

YIELD: 2 REGULAR LOAVES OR 4 MINI LOAVES

BLACK BOTTOM CUPCAKES

RECIPE FROM TERRISA SELL

METHOD

1. Preheat oven to 350 degrees. Prep a 12-cup muffin pan with cupcake liners. Set aside.
2. Mix the cream cheese, egg, 1/3 cup sugar, and 1/8 teaspoon salt in a small bowl until smooth. Gently stir in the chocolate morsels. Set aside.
3. In a large bowl, mix sifted flour, baking soda, baking cocoa, 1 teaspoon salt, and 1 cup sugar. Stir in water, oil, vinegar, and vanilla. Beat until blended.
4. Divide the cocoa batter into the 12 cupcake liners; each about 3/4 full. Top each with heaping dollops of the cream cheese mixture.
5. Bake for 25 to 30 minutes, until a toothpick or butter knife inserted into the chocolate cake comes out clean and the cream cheese center is set.
6. Let cool before removing cupcakes from their liners to eat, or they will stick to the lining.
7. To store, wrap tightly in plastic wrap or foil, or place them in a resealable plastic bag or an airtight container. Keep at room temperature.

INGREDIENTS

- 1 (8-ounce) package cream cheese, softened
- 1 large egg
- 1 and 1/8 teaspoons salt, divided
- 1 and 1/3 cups granulated sugar, divided
- 1 cup semi-sweet chocolate morsels
- 1 and 1/2 cups sifted all-purpose flour
- 1 teaspoon baking soda
- 1/4 cup baking cocoa
- 1 cup water
- 1/3 cup vegetable oil
- 1 tablespoon apple cider vinegar
- 1 teaspoon vanilla extract

YIELD: 12 CUPCAKES

Variations: Omit chocolate morsels completely from the cream cheese mixture for a more sweet versus savory Danish pastry vibe. You can also make smaller cupcakes by dividing the batter into two 12-cup muffin pans, making 24 cupcakes.

Young Wanda, seven or eight years old.

BLONDIES

RECIPE FROM CINDY SELL

METHOD

1. Preheat oven to 325 degrees. Line a 9x9-inch stainless steel baking dish with parchment paper. Set aside.
2. In a large bowl, mix softened butter and brown sugar.
3. Mix in the eggs and vanilla extract.
4. Mix in the flour, baking powder, and salt.
5. Gently stir in the butterscotch morsels and halved Rolo pieces.
6. Spread batter into the prepared baking dish.
7. Bake for about 40 minutes. It is done when a toothpick or knife inserted halfway between the edge and the center comes out with a few moist crumbs. The center may be slightly jiggly and will continue firming up as it cools.
8. Let cool before cutting into serving sizes, about 2x3-inch pieces, and eating.
9. To store blondies and keep them fresh and moist, wrap them tightly in plastic wrap or foil, then place them in an airtight container at room temperature for up to 5 days.

INGREDIENTS

- 1/2 cup (1 stick) butter, softened
- 1 and 1/2 cups brown sugar, firmly packed
- 2 eggs
- 1 teaspoon vanilla extract
- 2 and 1/4 cups all-purpose flour
- 2 teaspoons baking powder
- 1 teaspoon salt
- 1 (12-ounce) package of butterscotch morsels
- 3 (1.7-ounce) packs Rolo Creamy Caramels chocolate candies, unwrapped and halved

YIELD: ABOUT 12 BLONDIES

Variation: Use gluten-free all-purpose flour for a non-gluten treat.

BROWNIES WITH CHOCOLATE ICING

INGREDIENTS

- 1/2 cup (1 stick) butter, softened
- 1 cup granulated sugar
- 1 teaspoon salt
- 4 eggs
- 1 cup all-purpose flour
- 1 (24-ounce) bottle chocolate syrup
- 1 teaspoon vanilla extract
- 1 cup chopped nuts, optional
- 1 (10-ounce) package mini marshmallows

ICING

- 4 cups powdered sugar
- 1/2 cup (1 stick) butter, softened
- 2 tablespoons baking cocoa
- 1/3 cup milk
- 1 teaspoon vanilla extract

METHOD

1. Preheat oven to 325 degrees. Line a 13x9-inch baking dish with parchment paper. Set aside.
2. In a large bowl, mix the butter, sugar, and salt. Add eggs one at a time. Mix in the flour, chocolate syrup, vanilla extract, and nuts (if desired).
3. Pour batter into the prepared baking dish.
4. Bake for about 50 to 60 minutes. Insert a toothpick or butterknife halfway between the edge and center; if it comes out with a few moist crumbs (not batter), it's done.
5. As soon as you take the brownies out of the oven, while piping hot, sprinkle marshmallows all over the top, spread out slightly. Let cool completely.
6. While brownies are cooling, mix icing ingredients in a medium bowl.
   a. Mix butter and powdered sugar one cup at a time.
   b. Mix in baking cocoa, milk, and vanilla extract until smooth and creamy.
7. Once the brownie layer has cooled out of the oven, spread icing over the top of the marshmallows.
8. Cut into serving sizes, about 2x3-inch pieces.
9. To store brownies and keep them both fresh and moist, wrap them tightly in plastic wrap or foil, then place them in an airtight container in the fridge for up to 5 days.

YIELD: ABOUT 1 DOZEN PIECES

BUTTER COOKIES

INGREDIENTS

- 1 cup butter (2 sticks), softened
- 1/2 cup powdered sugar
- 2 cups all-purpose flour
- 1 teaspoon vanilla extract

METHOD

1. Preheat oven to 350 degrees. Line two large baking sheets with parchment paper. Set aside.
2. Add butter and sugar to a large bowl. Beat together until light and fluffy. The mixture should resemble whipped cream.
3. Mix in the flour and vanilla extract. The mixture will be crumbly at first, but should eventually form a thick, soft dough.
4. Break off pieces of dough and form rounds, about 1/2-inch in diameter.
5. Place cookies in the fridge for 30 minutes so the dough is chilled. This will prevent the cookies from spreading too much when they bake.
6. Once chilled, flatten them into discs with the palm of your hand; when baked, they will form an abstract flower shape.
7. Place one cookie sheet of flattened dough pieces in the middle of your oven. Bake cookies for about 15 minutes, or until the edges and surface turn a light brown. The flatter the cookies, the crispier they will be and the less time they need to bake.
8. Let cool on a wire rack before serving.
9. To store, place them in a resealable plastic bag or an airtight container. Keep at room temperature.

YIELD: ABOUT 4 DOZEN COOKIES

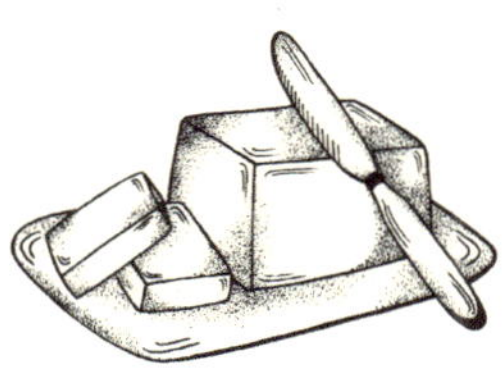

BUTTERMILK BISCUITS

METHOD

1. Preheat oven to 450 degrees. Line a baking sheet with parchment paper. Set aside.
2. In a large bowl, stir together flour, salt, and baking powder. Stir in shortening. Stir in milk.
3. Transfer to a floured board. Knead dough 10 to 12 strokes.
4. Roll out the dough and mold it into round shapes on the prepared baking sheet. They don't have to be perfect!
5. Bake for approximately 10 to 13 minutes. Check for doneness by gently touching the surface; they're likely done if they spring back slightly.
6. Let cool on a wire rack. Best served warm.
7. To store, wrap tightly in plastic wrap or foil, or place in a resealable plastic package or an airtight container. Keep at room temperature.

INGREDIENTS

- 2 cups all-purpose flour
- 3/4 teaspoon salt
- 4 teaspoons baking powder
- 1/3 cup shortening
- 2/3 cup milk or buttermilk

YIELD: 6 TO 8 BISCUITS

Pairs well with: Strawberry Jam (page 210) or Bacon Gravy (page 137).

BUTTERMILK PIE

RECIPE FROM CONNIE BEAM

PIE CRUST

INGREDIENTS

- 1 cup all-purpose flour
- 1/2 cup shortening
- 1/2 teaspoon salt
- 1/8 to 1/4 cup ice water

METHOD

1. Combine flour, shortening, and salt with a pastry cutter until shortening is in small, manageable chunks. Do not overwork the dough.
2. Slowly add in ice water with one hand while continuing to form the dough into a ball with the other hand. Use as much ice water as needed until the dough comes together nicely into a ball. Do not overwork the dough.
3. Flour your countertop or breadboard. Put the dough on the floured surface and shape into a ball.
4. Flatten the ball into a disk. Sprinkle flour on top of the dough. Roll out with a rolling pin to the desired size.
5. Line a pie pan with the dough and pinch out the crust.

METHOD

1. Prepare pie crust.
2. Preheat oven to 350 degrees.
3. Mix butter, sugar, flour, eggs, buttermilk, and vanilla extract in a large bowl and pour into the uncooked pie crust. Fill the pie crust very full; it will bake and cool down in size. You may still have some extra filling.
4. Bake for 45 to 50 minutes. If the center of the pie is still a little jiggly, you'll need to bake a little longer, checking on the pie every 5 minutes or so.
5. Let cool.
6. Store covered on the counter or in the fridge for up to 5 days.

INGREDIENTS

- 1 uncooked pie crust
- 1/4 cup (1/2 stick) butter, melted
- 2 cups granulated sugar
- 3 tablespoons all-purpose flour
- 3 eggs
- 1 cup buttermilk
- 1 teaspoon vanilla extract

YIELD: 8 SERVINGS

BUTTERSCOTCH PRALINE

INGREDIENTS

- 1 (3.4-ounce) package instant butterscotch pudding and pie filling mix
- 1 cup granulated sugar
- 1/2 cup firmly packed brown sugar
- 1/2 cup evaporated milk
- 1 tablespoon butter, softened
- 1 and 1/2 cup chopped pecans

METHOD

1. Line a large baking sheet with parchment paper. Set aside.
2. Mix the first five ingredients in a large, heavy saucepan. Bring to a boil.
3. Cook over medium heat, stirring occasionally, until the mixture reaches a soft ball stage, 234 degrees on a candy thermometer. At this stage, if a small amount of the syrup is dropped into cold water, it will form a soft, pliable ball that can be flattened.
4. Remove from the heat and add in pecans. Stir vigorously with a wooden spoon for 2 to 3 minutes or until the mixture is creamy and begins to thicken.
5. Working rapidly, drop rounded tablespoonfuls onto the prepared baking sheet. Let cool on the counter at room temperature before eating.
6. Store in an airtight container.

YIELD: ABOUT 1 DOZEN

Recommendation: A candy thermometer is helpful for this recipe, but not necessary.

Teenage Wanda, mid 1940s.

CANDY CANE COOKIES

METHOD

1. In a small bowl, mix granulated sugar with crushed peppermint candies. Set aside.
2. In a large bowl, mix butter, powdered sugar, egg, almond and vanilla extract.
3. Sift flour and salt and stir into the butter mixture.
4. Divide and remove half the batter from the bowl, set aside. Add red food coloring to the remaining dough in the bowl. Mix until the color is evenly distributed.
5. Pat each piece of dough into a disk, wrap in plastic wrap, and refrigerate for at least 3 hours or overnight.
6. Preheat oven to 375 degrees. Line a baking sheet with parchment paper.
7. In 1 to 2-inch increments, pinch off dough from each color and gently roll out, 4 inches long.
8. Place rolled strips side by side, gently twist them like a rope, and shape them into a candy cane shape.
9. Place on prepared baking sheet and bake for 9 to 12 minutes.
10. While hot out of the oven, sprinkle with sugar and peppermint mixture.
11. Store in an airtight container.

INGREDIENTS

- 1/2 cup granulated sugar
- 1/2 cup crushed peppermint candy
- 1/2 cup (1 stick) butter
- 1 cup powdered sugar
- 1 egg
- 1 and 1/2 teaspoon almond extract
- 1 teaspoon vanilla extract
- 1 and 1/2 cups all-purpose flour
- 1 teaspoon salt
- 1/2 teaspoon red food coloring

YIELD: 2 TO 3 DOZEN COOKIES

CARROT CAKE

METHOD

1. Preheat oven to 350 degrees. Grease and flour the bottoms and sides of three 8- to 9-inch cake pans. Set aside.
2. In a large bowl, mix sugar and vegetable oil, then mix in eggs.
3. Mix sifted dry ingredients into the above. Stir in grated or finely chopped carrots and nuts.
4. Divide the cake batter evenly between the prepared cake pans and bake for about 40 to 45 minutes, until the tops of the cake layers are springy when touched or when a toothpick or butter knife inserted into the center of the cake comes out clean.
5. While cakes are baking, mix frosting ingredients in a medium bowl and set aside.
6. Let the cakes cool in their pans for at least 15 minutes, then carefully place the cake layers onto cooling racks.
7. When the cake layers are completely cool, frost the top of one layer, and repeat frosting the tops of the second and third layer as you stack them, leaving the sides exposed.
8. Sprinkle the top with a handful of nuts. Cut into 12 to 16 equally sized pieces.
9. Frosted carrot cake lasts in the fridge for up to 1 week, covered.

YIELD: 12 TO 16 SLICES

INGREDIENTS

- 2 cups sugar
- 1 and 1/2 cups vegetable oil
- 4 eggs, well-beaten
- 2 teaspoons baking soda
- 2 cups all-purpose flour
- 2 teaspoons cinnamon
- 1 teaspoon salt
- 3 cups grated or finely chopped carrots
- 1 cup chopped nuts, more for garnishing

FROSTING

- 1/2 cup (1 stick) margarine, softened
- 4 cups powdered sugar
- 2 (8-ounce) packages cream cheese, softened
- 1 teaspoon fresh lemon juice

CHERRY PIE

INGREDIENTS

- 2 unbaked pie crusts
- 2 (14.5-ounce) cans pitted tart cherries in water
- 1/4 cup cornstarch
- 1 and 1/2 cups granulated sugar
- 1 tablespoon butter
- 2 tablespoons fresh lemon juice

PIE CRUST

INGREDIENTS

- 2 cups all-purpose flour
- 1 cup shortening
- 1 teaspoon salt
- 1/4 to 1/3 cup ice water

METHOD

1. Combine flour, shortening, and salt with a pastry cutter until shortening is in small, manageable chunks. Do not overwork the dough.
2. Slowly add in ice water with one hand while continuing to form the dough into a ball with the other hand. Use as much ice water as needed until the dough comes together nicely into a ball. Do not overwork the dough.
3. Flour your countertop or breadboard. Put the dough on the floured surface and shape into a ball. Cut in half, one piece for each pie crust.
4. Flatten the first dough half into a disk. Sprinkle flour on top of the dough. Roll out with a rolling pin to the desired size.
5. Line a pie pan with the dough and pinch out the crust.
6. Flatten the second dough half into a disk. Sprinkle flour on top of the dough. Roll out with a rolling pin to the desired size. Cut dough into 1/2 to 3/4-inch wide strips to create a lattice pattern on top of the pie.

CHERRY PIE

METHOD

1. Prepare pie crusts.
2. Preheat oven to 400 degrees.
3. Drain juice from both cans of cherries into a small bowl.
4. In a separate small bowl, mix the cornstarch and 1/3 cup of the drained cherry juice, and set aside.
5. Heat the saucepan full of the remaining cherry juice over medium heat. Add in sugar and stir well. Bring the mixture to a low boil.
6. Stir in the cornstarch and cherry juice mixture. Cook, stirring, until slightly thicker, about 2 to 3 minutes.
7. Stir in butter and fresh lemon juice. Gently stir in the cherries. Remove from heat.
8. Allow the mixture to cool to room temperature, and pour into the pie crust base. Create a lattice pattern for the top pie crust and sprinkle with granulated sugar.
9. Bake for 15 to 20 minutes. Check on the pie. Cover the edges of the pie with aluminum foil or a pie crust shield so the edges of the pie crust do not burn. Lower the oven temperature to 375 degrees and bake for another 20 to 25 minutes.
10. Place the pie on a wire cooling rack and allow it to cool for several hours before serving at room temperature.
11. To store leftover cherry pie, cover it tightly with plastic wrap or aluminum foil and refrigerate for up to 4 days.

YIELD: ABOUT 8 SERVINGS

CHOCOLATE CHIP COOKIES

METHOD

1. In a medium bowl, mix sifted flour, baking soda, and salt. Set aside.
2. In a large bowl, beat together the butter and both sugars until the mixture is smooth and creamy.
3. Mix in eggs one at a time, along with the vanilla extract. Mix in the dry ingredients until combined.
4. Gently stir in the chocolate morsels last. The dough will be thick, so you may need to use your hands to mix.
5. Cover and put in the fridge. Chill the dough for 2 hours to overnight.
6. When you remove the dough from the fridge, let it sit on the counter for about 10 minutes.
7. Preheat oven to 375 degrees. Line a large baking sheet with parchment paper.
8. Bake in the oven for about 11 minutes. Chocolate chip cookies are done when the edges are golden brown and slightly set, while the center remains soft and puffy. They will continue to cook slightly as they cool, so remove them from the oven just before they appear fully cooked.
9. Store the cookies in an airtight container at room temperature for 3 to 7 days, in the fridge for up to 2 weeks, or freeze them for several months.

YIELD: ABOUT 5 DOZEN

INGREDIENTS

- 4 and 1/2 cups sifted all-purpose flour
- 2 teaspoons baking soda
- 1 and 1/2 teaspoons salt
- 2 cups (4 sticks) butter, softened
- 2 cups firmly packed brown sugar
- 1 cup granulated sugar
- 4 eggs
- 2 teaspoons vanilla extract
- 1 and 1/2 cups chocolate morsels

CHOCOLATE-COVERED CHERRIES

METHOD

1. Line a baking sheet with parchment paper. Set aside.
2. Drain maraschino cherries and dry them on absorbent paper towels.
3. In a large bowl, beat butter and gradually add sugar. Blend in milk and vanilla. Beat well until the mixture is similar to a thick frosting.
4. Glob a small amount of sugar mixture around each cherry. (If the mixture isn't dipping well, you can microwave for a few seconds to get a better consistency for coating.)
5. Place covered cherries on the prepared baking sheet. Chill in fridge for about 2 hours or until the coating is firm.
6. In a microwave-safe bowl, heat and stir the chocolate morsels and almond bark in 20 to 30-second bursts in a microwave until the morsels are melted and smooth.
7. Dip each cherry by the stem into the chocolate. If you notice the sugar coating is melting, you may need to work in batches, re-refrigerating half the cherries until cold and firm, then dipping them in chocolate.
8. Working quickly, place each cherry back on the prepared baking sheet. Chill in the fridge until firm.
9. Can last 1 to 2 weeks in the fridge in an airtight container.

INGREDIENTS

- About 48 maraschino cherries, with stems
- 1 and 1/4 cup (2 and 1/2 sticks) butter, melted
- 1/4 teaspoon vanilla extract
- 2 and 1/2 cups sifted powdered sugar
- 1 and 1/2 teaspoons milk
- 2-ounces (1/4 cup) semi-sweet chocolate morsels
- 1/3-pound white chocolate almond bark (also called vanilla candy coating), broken up

YIELD: ABOUT 4 DOZEN CHOCOLATE-COVERED CHERRIES

CHOCOLATE DELIGHT

RECIPE FROM CONNIE BEAM

METHOD

1. Preheat oven to 350 degrees. Set aside a 13x9-inch baking dish.
2. In a medium bowl, mix the crust ingredients by hand.
3. Cover the bottom of the baking dish with the mixture.
4. Bake for 15 to 20 minutes or until it reaches a light golden brown color.
5. Let cool.
6. While the crust is cooling, combine the following filling ingredients in a large bowl: cream cheese, sugar, and half of the whipped topping. Mix until smooth.
7. Spread mixture over cooled crust.
8. In a separate bowl, whisk together the pudding powders and milk until smooth.
9. Pour pudding over cream cheese mixture.
10. After the pudding has set, spread the remaining whipped topping on top.
11. Let the dessert chill in the fridge for at least 2 hours or overnight.
12. Serve cold.
13. Store, covered, in the fridge for up to 1 week.

YIELD: ABOUT 12 SERVINGS

INGREDIENTS

CRUST

- 3/4 cups (1 and 1/2 sticks) butter, softened
- 1 and 1/2 cups all-purpose flour

FILLING

- 1 (8-ounce) package cream cheese, softened
- 1 cup powdered sugar
- 1 (16-ounce) tub whipped topping, divided

PUDDING

- 1 small package (3.4-ounce) instant vanilla pudding mix
- 1 small package (3.9-ounce) instant chocolate pudding mix
- 4 cups cold milk

CHOCOLATE MAYONNAISE CAKE

CAKE FROM AUNT SALTY, FROSTING FROM GRANDMA BROWNE

METHOD

1. Preheat oven to 350 degrees. Grease and flour two 8- to 9-inch cake pans. Set aside.
2. In a large bowl, sift together the dry ingredients.
3. Blend in mayonnaise, water, and vanilla extract.
4. Divide the batter evenly into the two prepared cake pans.
5. Bake for approximately 25 minutes, until a toothpick or butter knife inserted in the center of the cake comes out clean.
6. Let cool before turning over on a cooling rack.
7. While cooling, make the glaze: Combine powdered sugar, evaporated milk, and unsweetened chocolate in a saucepan. Cook over low heat, whisking until the sugar dissolves. Cook and whisk until smooth. Remove from the heat, add butter, and whisk until well combined. Let the sauce cool until warm. Add vanilla and salt, and whisk again until the surface is smooth, about 3 minutes. Let it sit and cool.
8. Continue to let the cake and frosting cool completely before frosting. Frost the tops of each cake and layer on top of one another. Finish frosting sides of cake. Sprinkle nuts over the top.
9. Frosted cake can last covered in the fridge for up to 1 week.

YIELD: ABOUT 12 SERVINGS

INGREDIENTS

- 2 cups all-purpose flour
- 1 cup granulated sugar
- 1/2 cup baking cocoa
- 2 teaspoons baking soda
- 1/2 teaspoon salt
- 1 cup mayonnaise
- 1 cup warm water
- 1 teaspoon vanilla extract

FUDGE NUT FROSTING

- 3 cups powdered sugar
- 6 ounces (1/2 of a 12-ounce can) evaporated milk
- 2 squares of unsweetened chocolate, 1-ounce per square
- 1/4 cup butter
- 1 teaspoon vanilla extract
- 1/4 teaspoon salt
- Chopped nuts, for topping

CHOCOLATE PEANUT BUTTER BARS

INGREDIENTS

- 2 cups graham cracker crumbs
- 2 cups powdered sugar
- 1 cup (2 sticks) butter, softened
- 1 cup chunky peanut butter
- 1 (12-ounce) bag semi-sweet chocolate morsels
- 1/2-pound white chocolate almond bark (also called vanilla candy coating), broken up

METHOD

1. Line a 13x9-inch baking dish with parchment paper. Set aside.
2. Stir graham cracker crumbs, powdered sugar, softened butter, and chunky peanut butter in a large bowl.
3. Evenly distribute the peanut butter mixture into the bottom of the prepared baking dish.
4. In a microwave-safe bowl, heat and stir the chocolate morsels and almond bark in 20 to 30-second bursts in a microwave until the morsels are melted and smooth. Evenly pour and spread over the peanut butter layer.
5. Refrigerate for 1 to 2 hours.
6. Peel the parchment paper with the dessert out from the baking dish. Let sit on the counter until the dessert is close to room temperature and cut into desired serving sizes.
7. Store in the fridge for up to 5 days or in the freezer for up to 3 months in an airtight container.

YIELD: 12 TO 18 SQUARES

CHOCOLATE PEANUT BUTTER ROUNDS

INGREDIENTS

- 4 cups powdered sugar
- 2 cups (16-ounces) creamy peanut butter
- 1/2 cup butter, softened
- 1 teaspoon vanilla extract
- 12-ounces semi-sweet or dark chocolate morsels
- 1/2-pound white chocolate almond bark (also called vanilla candy coating), broken up

METHOD

1. Line a large baking sheet with parchment paper. Set aside.
2. Beat together sugar, peanut butter, butter, and vanilla extract in a large bowl until the mixture is smooth and creamy.
3. Roll this mixture into walnut-sized rounds, compact and dense, and place them on the prepared baking sheet.
4. Refrigerate the rounds for 3 to 4 hours until they are firm.
5. In a microwave-safe bowl, heat and stir the chocolate morsels and almond bark in 20- to 30-second bursts in a microwave until the morsels are melted and smooth.
6. Working quickly, dip chilled peanut butter balls into the melted chocolate, one at a time, to coat thoroughly. Place each round back on the parchment paper.
7. Cool for 1 to 2 hours in the fridge until the chocolate is set.
8. Store the peanut butter rounds in an airtight container in the fridge for up to 1 week or in the freezer for 2 to 3 weeks.

YIELD: ABOUT 3 DOZEN

Variation: For a vegan option, substitute the chocolate and unsalted butter for plant-based versions.

CHOCOLATE PIE

INGREDIENTS

- 2 baked pie crusts
- 2 cups granulated sugar
- 9 tablespoons all-purpose flour, leveled
- 1/2 cup baking cocoa
- 2 cups milk
- 1 (12-ounce) can evaporated milk
- 5 eggs, separated
- 2 teaspoons butter
- 2 teaspoons vanilla extract

MERINGUE

- 5 egg whites
- 1 teaspoon of granulated sugar for each egg white

METHOD

1. Prepare pie crusts.
2. Decrease oven temperature from 425 degrees from baking the pie crust down to 325 degrees.
3. Sift together dry ingredients (sugar, flour, and cocoa) in a medium bowl and set aside.
4. In a large saucepan, combine the milk, evaporated milk, and beaten egg yolks. Stir constantly over medium heat until the mixture begins to boil – be careful not to scorch it or let it cook on the bottom of the pan. When in doubt, keep stirring.
5. Remove the saucepan from heat and whisk in the dry ingredients.
6. Return to the stove on low heat and continue stirring until the mixture thickens to a pudding-like consistency.
7. When thickened, remove from heat and stir in the butter and vanilla extract until fully melted and incorporated.
8. Pour the hot chocolate filling into the cooled pie crusts.
9. Make meringue: Mix egg whites and sugar in a separate bowl. Soft peaks take 2 to 4 minutes, stiff peaks, which look like whipped cream, take 4 to 6 minutes.
10. Top pies with meringue. Make sure pie filling is hot when topping it with meringue – this helps seal the meringue to the filling and prevents weeping. Spread the meringue to the crust edges to seal it and prevent shrinking.
11. Bake for 10 to 15 minutes, watching closely after 10 minutes so the meringue doesn't over-brown.
12. Let the pie cool at room temperature for about 1 hour, then refrigerate to fully set for 3 to 5 hours.

CHOCOLATE PIE

PIE CRUST

INGREDIENTS

- 2 cups all-purpose flour
- 1 cup shortening
- 1 teaspoon salt
- 1/4 to 1/3 cup ice water

METHOD

1. Preheat oven to 425 degrees.
2. In a large bowl, combine flour, shortening, and salt with a pastry cutter until shortening is in small, manageable chunks. Do not overwork the dough.
3. Slowly add in ice water with one hand while continuing to form the dough into a ball with the other hand. Use as much ice water as needed until the dough comes together nicely into a ball. Do not overwork the dough.
4. Flour your countertop or breadboard. Put the dough on the floured surface and shape into a ball. Cut in half, one piece for each pie crust.
5. Flatten the first dough half into a disk. Sprinkle flour on top of the dough. Roll out with a rolling pin to the desired size.
6. Line a pie pan with the dough and pinch out the crust.
7. Repeat with the second dough half.
8. Poke the crust all over with a fork and apply pie weights.
9. Bake crusts for 10 to 15 minutes or until edges are slightly browned.
10. Take out the oven and let cool.

YIELD: 2 PIES, ABOUT 16 SERVINGS

Wanda, late teen years, late 1940s/early 1950s.

CHOCOLATE SWEET MILK CAKE

METHOD

1. Preheat oven to 350 degrees. Grease and flour 3 to 4 cake pans, 8 to 9 inches in diameter. Set aside.
2. In a large bowl, beat together shortening, sugar, chocolate, and eggs until the mixture is smooth and creamy.
3. Add milk to the chocolate mixture, alternating with flour, baking powder, and salt. Gently stir in nuts.
4. Pour into prepared cake pans.
5. Bake for about 24 to 30 minutes, until a toothpick or butter knife inserted in the center of the cake comes out clean.
6. While baking, combine the frosting ingredients in a separate large bowl and set aside.
7. Let the cake cool completely before frosting. Frost the tops of each cake and layer on top of one another. Finish frosting sides of cake. Sprinkle nuts over the top.
8. Cake lasts in the fridge for up to 1 week, covered.

YIELD: 12 TO 16 SLICES

INGREDIENTS

- 1/2 cup shortening
- 2 cups sugar
- 3 (1-ounce) squares semi-sweet baking chocolate, chopped and melted
- 2 eggs
- 1 and 1/2 cups sweet milk (whole milk)
- 2 cups all-purpose flour
- 2 teaspoons baking powder
- 1 pinch of salt
- 2 teaspoons vanilla extract
- 2 cups chopped nuts

FROSTING

- 1/4 cup (1/2 stick) butter, softened
- 3 squares unsweetened baking chocolate, 1-ounce per square, chopped and melted
- 2 cups powdered sugar
- 2 eggs
- 2 teaspoons fresh lemon juice
- 1 teaspoon salt
- 1 cup chopped nuts

CINDERELLA CAKE

RECIPE FROM CONNIE BEAM

METHOD

1. Preheat oven to 350 degrees. Grease and flour a fluted tube pan and set aside.
2. In a large bowl, beat the sugar and eggs. Add oil, mix.
3. In a separate medium bowl, combine the dry ingredients and then blend them into the egg mixture. Blend in the pumpkin.
4. Pour ingredients into the prepped fluted tube pan.
5. Bake for about 45 to 55 minutes, or until a toothpick or butter knife inserted into the center comes out clean, the cake is golden-brown, and the edges have begun to pull away from the sides of the pan.
6. Let cool before turning over onto a cooling rack.
7. While cooling, make icing in a large bowl by mixing cream cheese and butter, then mixing in powdered sugar and vanilla extract.
8. Once the cake has cooled, ice all sides of the cake.
9. To store, place the wrapped cake in a cool, dry area at room temperature.

YIELD: ABOUT 12 SLICES

INGREDIENTS

- 2 cups granulated sugar
- 4 eggs
- 1 cup vegetable oil
- 2 cups all-purpose flour
- 2 teaspoons baking soda
- 2 teaspoons cinnamon
- 1/2 teaspoon salt
- 1 (15-ounce) can pure pumpkin

FROSTING

- 1 (8-ounce) package cream cheese, softened
- 1 stick (1/2 cup) butter, softened
- 4 cups powdered sugar
- 1 teaspoon vanilla extract

CINNAMON ROLLS

INGREDIENTS

DOUGH

- 3/4 cup milk, warmed
- 1 (1/4-ounce) package instant yeast
- 1/4 cup granulated sugar
- 1/4 cup (1/2 stick) butter, melted and cooled
- 1 egg and 1 egg yolk
- 3 cups all-purpose flour
- 1 teaspoon salt

FILLING

- 2 tablespoons ground cinnamon
- 2/3 cup firmly packed brown sugar
- 1/2 cup (1 stick) butter, softened
- 1 cup chopped nuts, optional

GLAZE

- 2 cups powdered sugar
- 2 to 4 tablespoons milk

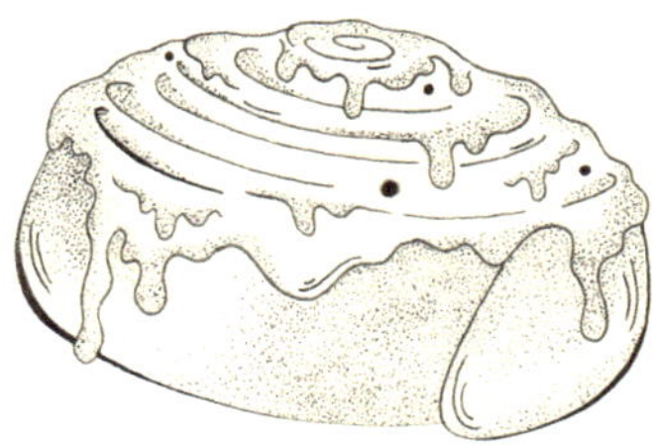

CINNAMON ROLLS

METHOD

1. Have a warm towel on standby. Grease a large bowl and set aside. Line a 9x9-inch baking dish with parchment paper and set aside.
2. Put the warmed milk in a separate large bowl. Add instant yeast and sugar, and let sit for about 5 minutes.
3. Add the butter, egg, yolk, and salt. Mix until well combined. Slowly stir in the flour until the dough forms.
4. Knead the dough on a well-floured surface for about 8 minutes. Put the dough in the reserved buttered bowl, cover with plastic wrap, and cover with the warmed towel.
5. Allow the dough to sit and rise for an hour to an hour and a half.
6. While rising, prepare the cinnamon filling by stirring together cinnamon and brown sugar in a small bowl. Set aside.
7. Once the dough is ready, place it on a well-floured surface. Roll the dough out flat with a rolling pin to about 12x18 inches. Rewarm the towel and set aside.
8. Spread the softened butter (not melted) onto the flattened dough. Sprinkle and rub the cinnamon and brown sugar mixture into the butter. Sprinkle the nuts evenly over the top, if using.
9. Roll the dough into a tight log shape. After rolling, close up the ends with your hands and condense the log, as it may have stretched out while rolling.
10. Cut into 1 to 1 and 1/2-inch sections, 12 rounds total.
11. Place dough rounds onto the prepared baking dish, all snuggled up next to each other. Cover with plastic wrap and the warm towel again for about 1 more hour.
12. Preheat oven to 350 degrees.
13. Remove the towel and plastic wrap. Bake the rolls in the oven on the center rack for about 18 to 22 minutes.
14. While baking, make the glaze by mixing powdered sugar and milk in a medium-sized bowl.
15. Once rolls are slightly cooled, frost with glaze.
16. Serve warm.
17. To store, cover leftover frosted or unfrosted rolls tightly and keep at room temperature for up to 2 days or in the fridge for up to 5 days.

YIELD: 1 DOZEN ROLLS

Wanda's senior photo circa 1951.

COCONUT CREAM PIE

INGREDIENTS

- 1 parbaked pie crust
- 3/4 cup granulated sugar
- 1/3 cup all-purpose flour
- 1/4 teaspoon salt
- 1 and 1/2 cups scalded milk
- 3 eggs, separated
- 2 tablespoons butter
- 1 teaspoon vanilla extract
- 2 cups sweetened flaked coconut, divided (1 cup in the filling and 1 cup toasted in the oven)

PIE CRUST

INGREDIENTS

- 1 cup all-purpose flour
- 1/2 cup shortening
- 1/2 teaspoon salt
- 1/8 to 1/4 cup ice water

METHOD

1. Preheat oven to 425 degrees.
2. Combine flour, shortening, and salt with a pastry cutter until shortening is in small, manageable chunks. Do not overwork the dough.
3. Slowly add in ice water with one hand while continuing to form the dough into a ball with the other hand. Use as much ice water as needed until the dough comes together nicely into a ball. Do not overwork the dough.
4. Flour your countertop or breadboard. Put the dough on the floured surface and shape into a ball.
5. Flatten the dough into a disk. Sprinkle flour on top of the dough. Roll out with a rolling pin to the desired size.
6. Line a pie pan with the dough and pinch out the crust. Since you are parbaking the crust, prick all over the bottom and sides of the pie crust with a fork and bake using pie weights.
7. Bake for 15 to 20 minutes.

COCONUT CREAM PIE

METHOD

1. In the upper part of a double boiler, mix sugar, flour, and salt. Gradually stir in milk. Stir until the mixture thickens, about 10 minutes.
2. Remove from the heat, stir in well-beaten egg yolks, return the pan to the boiling water, and cook for 2 more minutes, stirring constantly.
3. Add butter and vanilla.
4. Stir 1 cup flaked coconut into the cream filling.
5. Pour warm filling into cooled pie crust. Cover tightly with plastic wrap directly on the surface of the pudding and refrigerate for at least 3 hours or overnight until chilled and thickened.
6. Preheat oven to 350 degrees.
7. Top with Meringue: 1 teaspoon of sugar per egg white. Beat until the egg whites form peaks, then top the pie.
8. Sprinkle the top with the remaining toasted coconut.
9. Bake for 15 minutes or until delicately browned.
10. Chill the pie uncovered up to a few hours, or you can serve it immediately.
11. Cover leftovers and store in the fridge for up to 5 days.

YIELD: 8 SERVINGS

COFFEE ANGEL FOOD CAKE

INGREDIENTS

- 1 and 2/3 cups egg whites (about 1 dozen large eggs)
- 1 teaspoon vanilla extract
- 1 and 1/2 teaspoons cream of tartar
- 1 and 3/4 cups sifted granulated sugar, divided
- 1 tablespoon powdered instant coffee
- 1 cup plus 2 tablespoons all-purpose flour

COFFEE BUTTER ICING

- 1/2 cup (1 stick) butter, softened
- 2 and 1/2 cups sifted powdered sugar
- 2 to 3 tablespoons milk
- 1 tablespoon instant coffee (dissolved in 1 tablespoon hot water)
- 1 teaspoon vanilla extract
- 1 cup raw almonds, sliced, for toasting

Recommendation: Save egg yolks to make up to three batches of Homemade Peach Ice Cream (page 79).

To store egg yolks: For every 4 egg yolks, add 1 and 1/2 teaspoons of sugar. Whisk the yolks and sugar together until the sugar is fully incorporated and the mixture is smooth. Freeze in an airtight container.

COFFEE ANGEL FOOD CAKE

METHOD

1. Preheat oven to 350 degrees. Set aside a fluted tube pan. DO NOT grease or flour the pan.
2. In a large bowl, beat egg whites with vanilla and cream of tartar until stiff peaks form, which looks like whipped cream, and the whites are glossy. Set aside.
3. In a separate medium bowl, sift 3/4 cup sugar and instant coffee with the flour five times. Set aside.
4. Add the remaining cup of sugar to the beaten egg whites, beating in 2 tablespoons of sugar at a time, fifteen strokes between each beating. Gently stir in flour and sugar mixture in four additions, about twenty stirs each time, until all is used.
5. Pour into the ungreased pan and bake for about 30 to 35 minutes. The cake is done when it turns a golden brown and springs back when lightly touched. You can also insert a toothpick, or butter knife into the center, and if it comes out clean, the cake is done.
6. While the cake is cooling, make the icing: In a large bowl, beat together butter and sugar, adding a small amount of sugar at a time. Beat constantly until the mixture is smooth and creamy. Add milk, coffee, and vanilla extract. Beat until light and fluffy.
7. Remove cake from the oven and cool with the pan inverted on a cooling rack for 1 to 3 hours. Once cooled, run a knife around the edges of the cake and shimmy it out of the pan while inverted.
8. Make toasted almonds while the cake is cooling. Keep the oven temperature at 350 degrees and line a baking pan with parchment paper. Spread the almonds in a single layer on the prepared pan. Bake the sliced almonds for 7 to 8 minutes, stirring every few minutes, or until golden brown. Immediately transfer the almonds to a plate to cool in a single layer.
9. Cover the cooled cake with icing and toasted almonds.
10. Make sure your cake is fully cooled to room temperature before storing it. You can wrap it with plastic wrap, place it on a cake plate with a dome or in a large sealable container. Your cake will last 1 to 2 days at room temperature or 1 week in the fridge.

YIELD: 12 TO 16 SERVINGS.

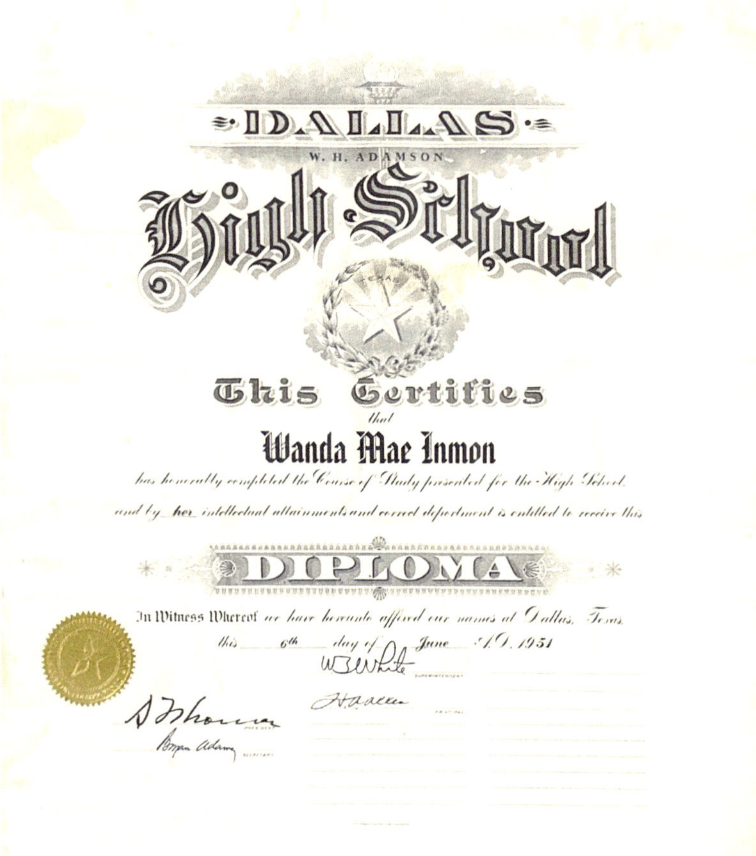

Wanda's High School diploma. June 6, 1951.

COFFEE CAKE

METHOD

1. Preheat oven to 350 degrees. Grease a fluted tube pan. Set aside.
2. Mix cake mix, instant pudding package, oil, eggs, water, vanilla extract, and butter extract in a large bowl on high speed for 8 minutes. Set aside.
3. In a separate bowl, stir together the filling ingredients.
4. Layer batter in thirds and put mixed filling on top of the first two layers.
5. Bake for approximately 50 minutes. The cake is done when a toothpick or knife comes out clean without batter.
6. Cool for 8 minutes in the pan, then remove the cake to a cooling rack.
7. While baking and cooling, stir the glaze ingredients together in a microwave-safe glass measuring cup with a pour spout. Set aside.
8. Once the cake has cooled, warm the glaze in the microwave and then drizzle it over the cake. Add more chopped pecans to the top if you'd like.
9. Make sure your cake is fully cooled to room temperature before storing it. You can wrap it with plastic wrap, place it on a cake plate with a dome, or in a large sealable container. Your cake will last up to 2 days at room temperature or 1 week in the fridge.

INGREDIENTS

- 1 package yellow cake mix
- 1 (8-ounce) package vanilla instant pudding mix
- 3/4 cup vegetable oil
- 4 eggs
- 3/4 cup water
- 1 teaspoon vanilla extract
- 1 teaspoon butter extract

FILLING

- 1/2 cup granulated sugar
- 4 teaspoons cinnamon
- 1/2 cup chopped pecans, plus more for topping, optional

GLAZE

- 1 cup powdered sugar
- 2 tablespoons milk
- 1/2 teaspoon butter extract

YIELD: 12 TO 16 SERVINGS

CREAMY DOUBLE DECKER FUDGE

RECIPE FROM AUNT DOT

METHOD

1. Line an 8-inch square pan with parchment paper. Set aside.
2. Place peanut butter morsels and the condensed milk in a small microwave-safe bowl. Microwave on high for 1 to 2 minutes, stirring after 1 minute, until chips melt when stirred.
3. Stir in 1/2 teaspoon vanilla extract and spread evenly into the prepared pan.
4. In a microwave-safe bowl, heat and stir the chocolate morsels and almond bark in 20- to 30-second bursts in a microwave until the morsels are melted and smooth.
5. Stir in the remaining 1/2 teaspoon vanilla extract and spread evenly over the peanut butter layer.
6. Refrigerate until firm, about 2 to 4 hours.
7. Flip the fudge over onto the cutting board, then peel away the paper. Cut into squares with the peanut butter side on top.
8. Store in an airtight container at room temperature for 2 to 3 weeks, preferably in a cool, dry location. Avoid refrigeration, as it can cause the fudge to dry out and become hard. For longer storage, you can freeze fudge for up to 1 year in an airtight container.

INGREDIENTS

- 1 cup peanut butter morsels
- 1 (14-ounce) can sweetened condensed milk
- 1 teaspoon vanilla extract, divided
- 12 ounces semi-sweet chocolate morsels
- 1/3 pound white chocolate almond bark (also called vanilla candy coating), broken up

YIELD: JUST UNDER 2 DOZEN

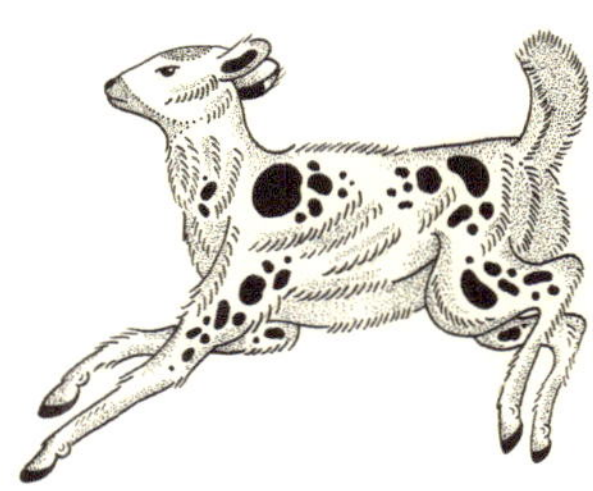

DATE ROUNDS

RECIPE FROM BARB SUTTON'S MOTHER, AGNES REDFAIR

METHOD

1. Line a baking sheet with parchment paper. Set aside.
2. Simmer egg, sugar, dates, and margarine or butter in a pan on medium to medium-high heat until the mixture thickens and reduces, about 5 minutes. You can continue to mash dates while they are simmering.
3. Remove from heat and stir in nuts, cereal, vanilla extract, and salt. Let cool.
4. Roll into walnut-sized balls and then roll in flaked coconut. Use a little margarine on your hands to help roll. Set on prepared baking sheet.
5. Cool in the fridge for 1 to 2 hours.
6. Store in the fridge, covered, for up to 1 week.

INGREDIENTS

- 1 egg
- 1 cup granulated sugar
- 1 and 1/2 cups (12-ounce) dates, chopped
- 1/2 cup (1 stick) margarine or butter
- 1/2 cup chopped nuts
- 3 cups crispy rice cereal
- 1 teaspoon vanilla extract
- 1/2 teaspoon salt
- Sweetened flaked coconut to coat

YIELD: ABOUT 2 DOZEN

DIVINITY CANDY

INGREDIENTS

- 2 large egg whites, room temperature
- 2 cups granulated sugar
- 1/2 cup water, with 2 tablespoons removed
- 1/2 cup light corn syrup
- 1 teaspoon vanilla extract
- 1 cup chopped nuts, if desired
- Butter, shortening, margarine, or cooking spray for spoon

Recommendation: Drop a candy into a hot cup of coffee for a unique take on cream and sugar.

DIVINITY CANDY

METHOD

1. Make this early in the morning or the day before.
2. Line a baking sheet with parchment paper. Set aside.
3. Beat egg whites in a medium bowl with an electric mixer on high speed until stiff peaks form, which looks like whipped cream. Set aside.
4. Cook sugar, water, corn syrup, and vanilla extract in a 2-quart saucepan over low heat, stirring constantly, until sugar is dissolved. Continue cooking on high heat, without stirring, until it reaches a rolling boil. Then, lower the temperature to medium to maintain a steady boil. When a small amount of the mixture is dropped into very cold water, it forms a hard ball that retains its shape while remaining pliable. If using a candy thermometer, it must reach 252 degrees. This may take longer than anticipated, and it is an important step, otherwise the batter will not set in step 5.
5. Remove from heat, allow boiling to stop, and pour sugar mixture into a glass measuring cup. Slowly pour the hot syrup into the egg whites in a thin stream. Continue beating on medium speed for at least 10 minutes, maintaining a constant speed. Do not stop mixing, even to scrape the bowl.
6. Beat until the mixture holds its shape in stiff peaks and becomes slightly dull. (Mixture may become too stiff for the mixer.)
7. Gently stir in nuts, if desired.
8. Drop the mixture from a greased spoon onto prepared baking sheet. Let the candies stand at room temperature for at least 12 hours, turning them over once, until they feel firm to the touch.
9. Packaged air-tight, candies will stay fresh at room temperature for 10 to 14 days.

YIELD: 2 TO 3 DOZEN CANDIES

Recommendation: A stand mixer and candy thermometer is helpful for this recipe, but not necessary.

FROZEN CHOCOLATE DESSERT

RECIPE FROM WYNONA CHASTAIN

INGREDIENTS

- 1 (12-ounce) can evaporated milk
- 1 (10-ounce) package mini marshmallows
- 6 ounces semi-sweet chocolate morsels
- 1/2 cup (1 stick) butter
- 1 cup sweetened flaked coconut
- 2 cups graham cracker crumbs
- 1/2 gallon (3 quarts) vanilla ice cream
- 1 cup chopped pecans

METHOD

1. Line a 13x9-inch baking dish with parchment paper. Set aside.
2. Combine the first three ingredients in a double boiler and bring water to a boil. Reduce the heat to low, and slowly cook while stirring, until all marshmallows and chocolate morsels are melted and the mixture is smooth. Remove from heat and set aside to cool.
3. Combine butter and coconut in a separate saucepan and cook, stirring often, until the coconut is slightly browned.
4. Remove from heat and stir in cracker crumbs. Let cool.
5. Press about 3/4 of the cooled crumb mixture into the prepared baking dish.
6. Cut half of the ice cream (1.5 quarts) into 1/2 inch-thick slices, and arrange these slices over the crumb mixture in the baking dish. Pour the cooled chocolate mixture over this first layer of ice cream.
7. Cut the remaining 1.5 quarts of ice cream into 1/2 inch-thick slices and arrange these slices over the chocolate mixture in the baking dish.
8. Combine the remaining crumb mixture and pecans. Sprinkle over the top of the dessert.
9. Cover and freeze until firm, at least 3 hours to overnight.
10. Cut into slices and serve cold.
11. Store in the freezer.

YIELD: 10 TO 12 SERVINGS

What's Cooking Good Looking
Wanda in the 1950s

FUDGE COOKIES

RECIPE FROM AUNT SALTY

METHOD

1. Preheat oven to 375 degrees. Line a baking sheet with parchment paper and set aside.
2. Sift flour, baking soda, salt, and baking cocoa into a large bowl. Add brown sugar, shortening, vanilla extract, milk, and eggs.
3. Beat 3 minutes on medium speed. Let batter stand for a few minutes.
4. Drop by imperfect heaping spoonfuls onto the prepared baking sheet.
5. Bake for 10 to 13 minutes. Don't overbake, or they will be dry. They should be the consistency of a moist mini brownie meets mini bread loaf, slightly undercooked in texture but not runny. They will continue to cook slightly while cooling down.
6. Mix the icing ingredients while the cookies bake. The melted butter must be piping hot to create the icing texture. It will be similar to cinnamon roll icing.
7. When cookies are done, let them sit for a few minutes on the pan, then transfer them to a cooling rack.
8. Ice cookies after they have cooled; don't stack until cold.
9. Store the cookies in an airtight container at room temperature for up to 7 days, in the fridge for up to 2 weeks, or freeze them for several months.

INGREDIENTS

- 3 cups all-purpose flour
- 1 and 1/2 teaspoons baking soda
- 1 and 1/2 teaspoons salt
- 2/3 cups baking cocoa
- 2 cups firmly packed brown sugar
- 3/4 cup shortening
- 2 teaspoons vanilla extract
- 1 and 1/3 cup milk
- 2 eggs

ICING

- 4 cups powdered sugar
- 1 cup (2 sticks) melted butter
- 3 teaspoons vanilla extract
- 1/4 teaspoon salt

YIELD: JUST UNDER 3 DOZEN

GERMAN CHOCOLATE CAKE

RECIPE FROM JACOBE SELL

INGREDIENTS

- 2 cups granulated sugar
- 1 and 3/4 cups all-purpose flour
- 3/4 cup baking cocoa
- 1 and 1/2 teaspoons baking powder
- 1 and 1/2 teaspoons baking soda
- 1 teaspoon salt
- 2 large eggs
- 1 cup buttermilk
- 1/2 cup vegetable oil
- 2 teaspoons vanilla extract
- 1 cup boiling water

COCONUT FROSTING

- 1/2 cup firmly packed brown sugar
- 1/2 cup granulated sugar
- 1/2 cup (1 stick) butter
- 3 large egg yolks, beaten
- 3/4 cup evaporated milk
- 1 tablespoon vanilla extract
- 1 cup chopped pecan halves
- 1 cup shredded sweetened coconut

CHOCOLATE BUTTERCREAM FROSTING

- 1/2 cup (1 stick) butter
- 2/3 cup baking cocoa
- 2 to 3 cups powdered sugar
- 1/3 cup evaporated milk
- 1 teaspoon vanilla extract

GERMAN CHOCOLATE CAKE

METHOD

1. Heat oven to 375 degrees. Grease two 9-inch round cake pans and set them aside.
2. Stir together sugar, flour, baking cocoa, baking powder, baking soda, and salt in a large bowl. Set aside.
3. Combine the eggs, buttermilk, oil, and vanilla extract in a separate bowl. Mix well.
4. Add the wet ingredients to the dry ingredients and mix until well combined.
5. Stir in boiling water; the batter will be very thin. Pour batter into prepared pans.
6. Bake for about 25 minutes until a toothpick or butter knife inserted in the center comes out clean. Let the mixture cool for 5 minutes in the pan, then transfer it to wire racks to cool completely.
7. While the cake is baking, make the frosting.
    a. Coconut Frosting: In a medium saucepan, add brown sugar, sugar, butter, egg yolks, and evaporated milk. Stir the mixture and bring it to a low boil over medium heat. Stir the mixture constantly for several minutes until it begins to thicken. Remove from heat and stir in vanilla, nuts, and coconut. Allow it to cool completely for 30 to 45 minutes, stirring occasionally, before frosting the cake.
    b. Chocolate Buttercream Frosting: Melt butter. Stir in baking cocoa. Add powdered sugar and milk in small amounts, alternating each. Beat until the mixture reaches a spreading consistency, then stir in the vanilla extract.
8. When the cake layers are completely cool, spread a thin layer of chocolate buttercream frosting over the first layer of the cake, then spoon half of the coconut frosting on top, spreading it into a smooth layer. Leave about 1/2 inch between the filling and the edge of the cake. Stack the second cake round on top. Spread smooth chocolate frosting evenly over the entire cake. Spoon the remaining coconut frosting on top of the cake.
9. You can decorate the cake with pecans, chopped or halved, and toasted coconut flakes.
10. Cake lasts in the fridge for up to 1 week, covered.

YIELD: 12 TO 16 SLICES

GRANNY APPLE PIE

RECIPE FROM TERRISA SELL

PIE CRUST

INGREDIENTS

- 1 cup all-purpose flour
- 1/2 cup shortening
- 1/2 teaspoon salt
- 1/8 to 1/4 cup ice water

METHOD

1. Combine flour, shortening, and salt with a pastry cutter until shortening is in small, manageable chunks. Do not overwork the dough.
2. Slowly add in ice water with one hand while continuing to form the dough into a ball with the other hand. Use as much ice water as needed until the dough comes together nicely into a ball. Do not overwork the dough.
3. Flour your countertop or breadboard. Put the dough on the floured surface and shape it into a ball.
4. Flatten the ball into a disk. Sprinkle flour on top, then roll out with a rolling pin to the desired size.
5. Line a pie pan with the dough and pinch out the crust.

INGREDIENTS

- 1 unbaked pie crust
- 2 pounds Granny Smith apples, grated
- 3 tablespoons all-purpose flour
- 3/4 cup granulated sugar
- 2 teaspoons cinnamon

TOPPING

- 1/2 cup (1 stick) butter, softened
- 1/3 cup brown sugar
- 2/3 cup all-purpose flour

METHOD

1. Prepare pie crust.
2. Preheat oven to 425 degrees.
3. Mix pie ingredients and pour them into the pie crust.
4. Mix the topping ingredients until crumbly and sprinkle and pat down over the top of the pie.
5. Bake for 20 minutes. Then lower the oven temperature to 400 degrees and bake for an additional 25 minutes.
6. Place the pie on a wire cooling rack. Serve warm.
7. To store leftover pie, cover it tightly with plastic wrap or aluminum foil and refrigerate for up to 4 days.

YIELD: ABOUT 8 SERVINGS

HOMEMADE PEACH ICE CREAM

RECIPE FROM CONNIE BEAM

METHOD

1. Dice peaches into small, bite-sized pieces.
2. Combine the peaches and the remaining ingredients in a medium saucepan. Warm over medium-low heat, whisking often, for 5 minutes, or until the sugar dissolves and the mixture is warm all the way through.
3. Pour into a heatproof bowl. Cover and chill in the fridge for 2 hours or overnight.
4. Pour the mixture into an ice cream churn and hand crank until it reaches a soft-serve consistency, meaning it's thick and holds its shape without being overly firm or watery. If you are using a home ice cream maker or stand mixer attachment, follow the instructions in the manual for how long to churn.
5. Serve cold.
6. Store in tubs in the freezer.

INGREDIENTS

- 2 cups peeled and pitted fresh or frozen peaches
- 4 egg yolks
- 1 and 1/2 cups granulated sugar
- 1 (12-ounce) can evaporated milk (full fat; fat-free won't work)

YIELD: 6 TO 8 SERVINGS

Recommendation: Blanching fresh peaches in hot water makes them easier to peel.

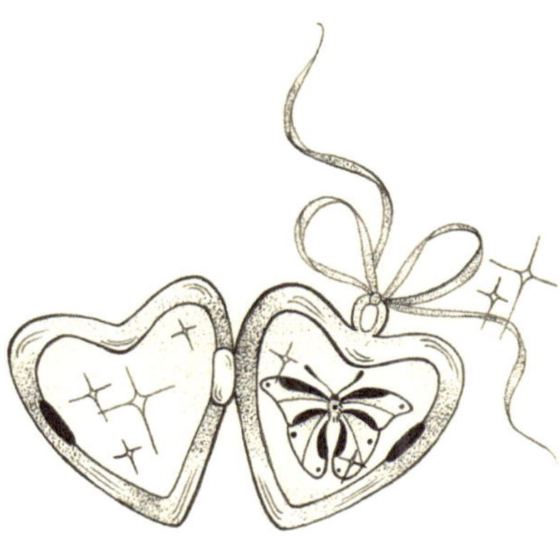

Wanda on the left with the "girls I worked with in Dallas."
1950s

ITALIAN CREAM CAKE

INGREDIENTS

- 2 cups granulated sugar
- 5 eggs, separated
- 1/2 cup (1 stick) margarine, softened
- 1/2 cup shortening
- 1 teaspoon baking soda
- 1 cup buttermilk
- 2 cups all-purpose flour
- 1 teaspoon vanilla extract
- 2 cups sweetened coconut shreds
- 1 cup chopped pecan halves, plus more for topping
- 1 to 2 cups coconut flakes for topping

FROSTING

- 1 (8-ounce) block cream cheese, softened
- 1/2 cup (1 stick) margarine, softened
- 4 cups powdered sugar
- 1 teaspoon vanilla extract

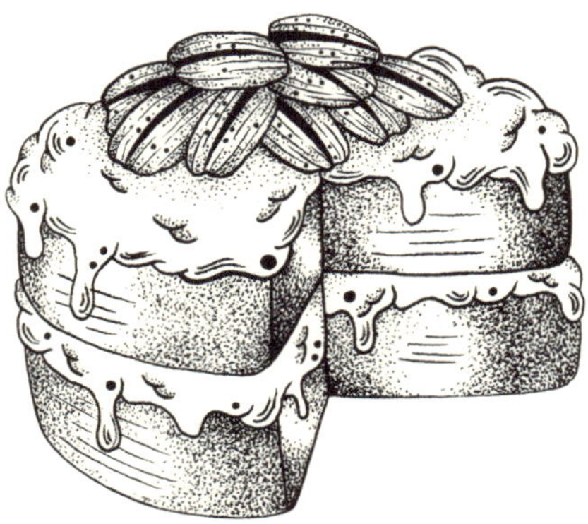

ITALIAN CREAM CAKE

METHOD

1. Preheat oven to 350 degrees. Grease and flour two to three 8- to 9-inch cake pans.
2. In a large bowl, beat egg whites until peaks form, which looks like whipped cream; set aside.
3. In a separate large bowl, mix the sugar and egg yolks until well combined.
4. Add margarine and shortening to this mixture, beating well.
5. In a separate small bowl, combine baking soda and buttermilk, add to the mixture alternately with flour, a little at a time.
6. Add the vanilla extract and coconut flakes. Gently stir in the stiffly beaten egg whites and chopped pecan halves.
7. Pour batter into the prepared cake pans.
8. Bake for approximately 30 to 40 minutes.
    - Closer to 30 minutes for three cake pans with less batter each.
    - Closer to 40 minutes for two full cake pans.
    - The cake is done when a toothpick or butter knife inserted in the center of the cake comes out clean, without batter.
    - If, after 30 minutes, the top sides of the cake are browning but the middle is gooey, you can cover the sides with aluminum foil while the center keeps baking.
9. While baking, mix frosting ingredients and set aside.
10. Let cakes cool before turning them onto a cooling rack.
11. When cool, frost the cake. Spread between layers and over the top and sides of the cake. Sprinkle with chopped pecan halves and toasted coconut flakes. To toast coconut flakes for the top of the cake, heat the oven to 325 degrees and put a thin layer on a baking sheet for 5 to 10 minutes until lightly browned, checking halfway through and giving a good shake.
12. Cake lasts in the fridge for up to 1 week, covered.

YIELD: 12 TO 16 SLICES

A vintage postcard advertising the hotel where Bob and Wanda met.

LEMON SQUARES

METHOD

1. Preheat oven to 350 degrees. Line an 8x8x2-inch pan or equivalent with parchment paper. The size of the pan is important to get the right thickness of the lemon squares. Set aside.
2. In a large bowl, mix flour, margarine, and powdered sugar.
3. Press the mixture into the pan and build up to 1/2-inch thick edges.
4. Bake for approximately 15 minutes; the crust should be just lightly browned.
5. While baking the crust, mix the remaining ingredients until light and fluffy.
6. Once the crust is done, set the dish on the counter for about 3 minutes, then pour the mixture over the hot crust.
7. Bake for 20 to 25 minutes until no indentations remain when touched lightly in the center.
8. Let cool before cutting. Sift a generous amount of powdered sugar on top before serving.
9. To store lemon bars, place them in an airtight container and refrigerate for up to 7 days, or freeze for up to 4 months.

INGREDIENTS

- 1 cup all-purpose flour
- 1/2 cup (1 stick) margarine or butter, softened
- 1/4 cup powdered sugar, more for dusting
- 2 eggs
- 1 cup granulated sugar
- 1/2 teaspoon baking powder
- 1/4 teaspoon salt
- 2 tablespoons fresh lemon juice
- 2 teaspoons grated lemon peel, optional

YIELD: ABOUT 1 DOZEN SERVINGS, DEPENDING ON HOW LARGE THE SQUARES ARE CUT.

MOUNTAIN DEW APPLE TURNOVERS

RECIPE FROM JANET KAY

METHOD

1. Preheat oven to 350 degrees. Grease a 13x9-inch baking dish. Set aside.
2. Separate the crescent rolls into triangles. Cut each apple into 8 slices, 16 slices total, to match the number of crescent roll triangle pieces.
3. Roll one piece of apple in each triangle of dough and place them in the prepared baking dish.
4. Mix both sugars, margarine, vanilla, and cinnamon in a large bowl until combined.
5. Pour the mixture over the rolls, then pour the Mountain Dew throughout the baking dish.
6. Bake for 35 to 40 minutes. The crescent rolls should be brown and crispy on top, but not burned. The underbelly will be slightly gooey, similar to the inside of a cinnamon roll.
7. Take the crescents out of the oven and let them cool. A soupy sauce will be at the bottom of the dish under the rolls. Crescents are best served warm with ice cream and some sauce spooned on top.

INGREDIENTS

- 2 (8-ounce) cans crescent rolls
- 2 Granny Smith apples
- 1 cup granulated sugar
- 1 cup firmly packed brown sugar
- 1 cup melted margarine
- 1 teaspoon vanilla extract
- 1 teaspoon cinnamon
- 1 can (12-ounce) Mountain Dew

YIELD: 16 ROLLS

NANAI(WANT)MO BARS

METHOD

1. Set aside an 8-inch baking pan lined with parchment paper.
2. Whisk butter, baking cocoa, and sugar for the base in the top of a double boiler. Once melted together, add the whisked egg and continue to whisk the mixture until it resembles custard. Remove from heat.
3. In a separate large bowl, mix the graham cracker crumbs, coconut, and pecans. Pour the baking cocoa mixture over these dry ingredients. Mix well with your hands until thoroughly combined, then press the mixture tightly into the base of the prepared pan.
4. For the middle layer, in a large bowl beat together butter, milk, vanilla pudding powder, and powdered sugar until the mixture is smooth and creamy. Spread over the base. Chill in the fridge for at least 1 hour.
5. Once the first two layers have chilled, create the topping by pouring the morsels and broken-up almond bark into a microwave-safe bowl. Heat in 20 to 30-second bursts in the microwave, stirring in between, until melted and well combined. Pour over the middle layer.
6. Let it set at room temperature until cool, then chill for several hours in the fridge.
7. Cut into squares to serve. Store in the fridge for up to 4 days, covered.

YIELD: 16 BARS

INGREDIENTS

BASE

- 1 egg, whisked
- 1/2 cup (1 stick) butter
- 5 tablespoons baking cocoa
- 1/4 cup granulated sugar
- 1 and 3/4 cups graham cracker crumbs
- 1 cup sweet coconut flakes
- 1/2 cup finely chopped pecans

MIDDLE LAYER

- 1/2 cup (1 stick) butter, softened
- 1/2 cup milk
- 1 (3.4-ounce) package instant vanilla pudding powder mix
- 4 cups powdered sugar, sifted

TOPPING

- 1 (12-ounce) bag semi-sweet chocolate morsels
- 1/2 pound white chocolate almond bark (also called vanilla candy coating), broken up

NORTHERN CORNBREAD

RECIPE FROM MARIJA GERBYA

METHOD

1. Preheat oven to 350 degrees. Grease and flour a 10- to 12-inch cast-iron skillet. Set aside.
2. In a large bowl, mix all ingredients.
3. Pour mixture into the prepared cast-iron skillet.
4. Bake for 40 to 45 minutes.
5. The bread is done when a toothpick or butter knife inserted in the center of the skillet comes out clean.
6. Serve warm.

INGREDIENTS

- 1/2 cup (1 stick) butter, softened
- 4 tablespoons granulated sugar
- 1 cup buttermilk
- 1/4 cup sour cream
- 3 eggs
- 2 (8.5-ounce) boxes Jiffy Corn Muffin Mix

YIELD: 8 TO 10 SLICES

Recommendation: Top with butter and honey, serve warm.

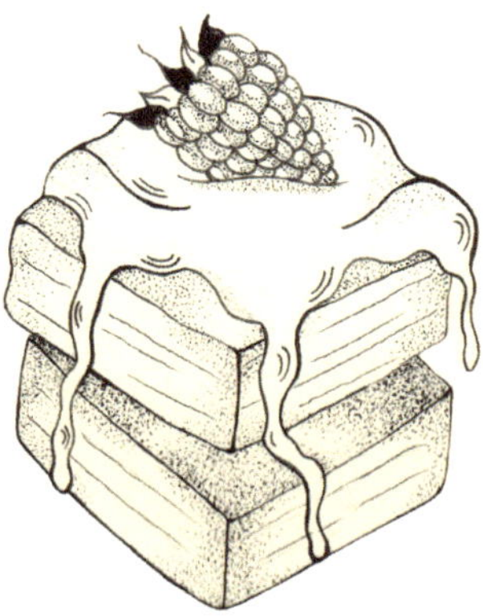

OATMEAL CHOCOLATE CHIP COOKIES

INGREDIENTS

- 2 cups (4 sticks) butter, softened
- 2 cups granulated sugar
- 2 cups firmly packed brown sugar
- 4 eggs
- 2 teaspoons vanilla extract
- 5 cups whole oats, blended to a fine powder
- 4 cups all-purpose flour
- 1 teaspoon salt
- 2 teaspoons baking powder
- 2 teaspoons baking soda
- 1 (24-ounce) package semi-sweet chocolate morsels
- 2 (4-ounce) frozen dark chocolate bars, grated or finely chopped
- 3 cups chopped toasted nuts
- Sea salt, for the tops of each cookie

METHOD

1. Preheat oven to 375 degrees. Line a baking sheet with parchment paper. Set aside.
2. In a large bowl, beat together the butter and both sugars until smooth and creamy. Mix in eggs and vanilla.
3. Measure out oats and blend in a blender to make a fine powder. Mix into your wet ingredient bowl, along with the flour, salt, baking powder, and baking soda. The mixture may become too thick for a mixer.
4. Gently stir in chocolate morsels, grated chocolate bar, and nuts. You may need to use your hands to mush all of the oats, chocolate, and nuts into the dough.
5. Roll into rounds and place 2 inches apart on the prepared baking sheet.
6. Bake for 10 to 14 minutes, rotating the tray halfway through. Cookies are done when the edges are golden brown and slightly cracked, the center looks set, not jiggly, but still soft.
7. Slam the tray on the counter when out of the oven to slightly flatten the cookies, then transfer them to a cooling rack. Add a pinch of sea salt to the top of each cookie.
8. Eat and enjoy.
9. Store cookies in an airtight container at room temperature for up to 4 days or in the freezer for up to 3 months.

YIELD: ABOUT 5 DOZEN

OATMEAL FUDGE COOKIES

METHOD

1. Line a baking sheet with parchment paper. Set aside.
2. Mix the oats, vanilla extract, and pecans in a large bowl. Set aside.
3. Mix sugar, baking cocoa, milk, and margarine in a medium saucepan. Bring the mixture to a rolling boil. Remove the saucepan from the heat and pour over the first mixture. Mix until well combined. You may need to use your hands to mush all of the oats in with the warm chocolate mixture.
4. Drop heaping spoonfuls of the mixture onto the prepared baking sheet. Refrigerate for 4 to 6 hours.
5. To store no-bake cookies, place them in an airtight container for up to 1 week in the fridge, or freeze them in a freezer-safe container for up to 3 months.

INGREDIENTS

- 3 cups uncooked old-fashioned oats
- 1 teaspoon vanilla extract
- 1 cup chopped pecans
- 2 cups granulated sugar
- 1/2 cup baking cocoa
- 1/2 cup milk
- 1/2 cup (1 stick) margarine

YIELD: 1 TO 2 DOZEN COOKIES

OATMEAL RAISIN COOKIES

RECIPE FROM KIM MARIE DORE-HACKBARTH

METHOD

1. Preheat oven to 350 degrees. Line a cookie sheet with parchment paper. Set aside.
2. In a large bowl, mix shortening and sugars until creamy. Mix in the eggs and vanilla extract. Set aside.
3. In a separate large bowl, sift together the flour, salt, and baking soda. Gently stir into the creamy mixture.
4. Stir in oats, raisins, and nuts (if using). You may need to use your hands to mush all of the oats in with the dough.
5. Roll into balls and place on the prepared cookie sheet. Flatten slightly with a fork.
6. Bake for 10 to 12 minutes until light brown.
7. Store in an airtight container on the counter for up to 1 week or in the freezer for up to 3 months.

INGREDIENTS

- 1 cup shortening
- 1 cup granulated sugar
- 1 cup brown sugar, firmly packed
- 2 eggs
- 1 teaspoon vanilla extract
- 1 and 1/2 cup all-purpose flour
- 1 teaspoon salt
- 1 teaspoon baking soda
- 3 cups quick oats
- 1 cup raisins
- 1 cup chopped nuts, optional

YIELD: 3 TO 4 DOZEN COOKIES

ORANGE ROUNDS

INGREDIENTS

- 1 (11-ounce) box Nilla Wafers
- 4 cups powdered sugar
- 6 ounces (3/4 cup) canned frozen orange juice, thawed
- 1/2 cup margarine, softened
- 1/2 cup nuts, finely chopped
- 1 and 1/2 cup sweetened flaked coconut

METHOD

1. Cover a large baking sheet with parchment paper. Set aside.
2. Place a handful of Nilla Wafers in a resealable zip-top bag and crush them with a rolling pin. Repeat with the remaining cookies.
3. Mix wafer crumbs, sugar, orange juice, and softened margarine in a large bowl.
4. Form into walnut-sized balls.
5. Roll half the rounds in sweetened flaked coconut and the other half in finely chopped nuts. Place on prepared baking sheet.
6. Put the uncovered parchment-lined baking sheet in the fridge and chill overnight to firm.
7. Serve cold.
8. Store in an airtight container and keep refrigerated or freeze.

YIELD: ABOUT 3 DOZEN

PEACH COBBLER

INGREDIENTS

- 1/2 cup margarine, melted
- 1 cup all-purpose flour
- 1 cup granulated sugar
- 2 teaspoons baking powder
- 2 teaspoons salt
- 3/4 cup milk
- 5 fresh or frozen peaches, peeled, cored, and sliced (about 4 cups); if using canned peaches 2 (15-ounce) cans, drained

METHOD

1. Preheat oven to 375 degrees.
2. Pour melted margarine into a 13x9-inch baking dish.
3. Mix the next five ingredients in a large bowl and pour into the baking dish over the melted butter.
4. Evenly pour fruit over the mixture.
5. Bake for 60 minutes, then turn up the oven to 425 degrees and bake for 10 more minutes until the crust turns a golden brown.
6. Serve warm.
7. Store leftover cobbler covered in the fridge for 4 to 5 days.

YIELD: 8 TO 9 SERVINGS

Variation: Make a blueberry cobbler instead with 4 cups frozen or fresh blueberries.

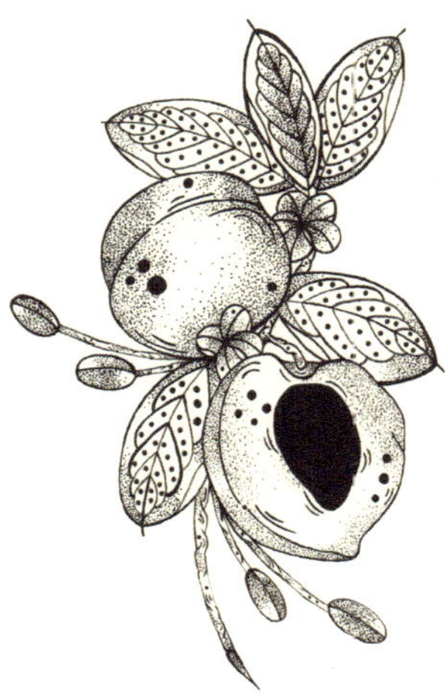

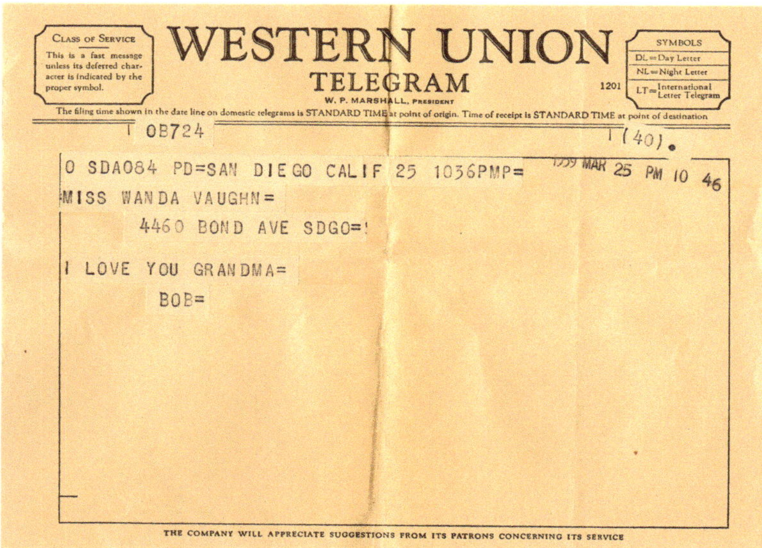

CLASS OF SERVICE
This is a fast message unless its deferred character is indicated by the proper symbol.

WESTERN UNION
TELEGRAM
W. P. MARSHALL, PRESIDENT

SYMBOLS
DL=Day Letter
NL=Night Letter
LT=International Letter Telegram

1201

The filing time shown in the date line on domestic telegrams is STANDARD TIME at point of origin. Time of receipt is STANDARD TIME at point of destination

OB724 (40).

O SDA084 PD=SAN DIEGO CALIF 25 1036PMP= 1959 MAR 25 PM 10 46
MISS WANDA VAUGHN=
4460 BOND AVE SDGO=
I LOVE YOU GRANDMA=
BOB=

THE COMPANY WILL APPRECIATE SUGGESTIONS FROM ITS PATRONS CONCERNING ITS SERVICE

Bob sent Wanda dozens of dozens of letters over the years. This is a very early telegram from Bob to Wanda. Wanda was about nine months older than Bob; he affectionately called her Grandma.

PEANUT BLOSSOM COOKIES

METHOD

1. Preheat oven to 375 degrees. Line a baking sheet with parchment paper. Set aside.
2. Sift together flour, baking soda, and salt. Set aside.
3. In a large bowl, beat together shortening, peanut butter, and both sugars until the mixture is smooth and creamy.
4. Mix in egg, milk, and vanilla extract.
5. Gradually combine the dry ingredients and mix thoroughly.
6. Shape dough into walnut-sized balls. Roll in sugar.
7. Put on the prepared baking sheet.
8. Bake for 8 minutes.
9. Remove from the oven and place a chocolate kiss in the center. Press in place so that each cookie cracks.
10. Bake for about 2 to 3 minutes longer.
11. Let cool.
12. To store, allow the cookies to cool completely to keep the chocolate center intact. Then, transfer the cookies to an airtight container and store at room temperature for up to 3 days.

INGREDIENTS

- 1 and 3/4 cups sifted all-purpose flour
- 1 teaspoon baking soda
- 1/2 teaspoon salt
- 1/2 cup shortening
- 1/2 cup peanut butter
- 1/2 cup granulated sugar, plus more for rolling
- 1/2 cup firmly packed brown sugar
- 1 egg
- 2 tablespoons milk
- 1 teaspoon vanilla extract
- 1 (10-ounce) package chocolate kisses

YIELD: ABOUT 3 DOZEN

PEANUT BRITTLE

METHOD

1. Preheat oven to 200 degrees. Grease a large baking sheet with butter and keep it warm in the oven.
2. In a small ramekin-sized bowl, mix baking soda, 1 teaspoon of water, and vanilla extract. Add in 1 teaspoon of butter. Set aside.
3. Mix sugars, 1 cup water, and corn syrup in a medium saucepan. Cook over medium-high heat, stirring occasionally, until a small amount of syrup dropped into frigid water forms a soft ball that flattens when removed from the water, or the temperature reaches 245 degrees on a candy thermometer.
4. Pour in the peanuts. Cook, stirring constantly, until a small amount of the mixture dropped into frigid water separates into hard, brittle threads, or the temperature reaches 295 degrees on a candy thermometer.
5. Immediately remove from heat. Quickly stir in the teaspoon of butter and the baking soda mixture until light and foamy.
6. Pour the candy mixture onto the warmed baking sheet, quickly spreading it about 1/4 inch thick. Cool completely, at least 1 hour at room temperature.
7. Break into pieces. Store in a covered container at room temperature.

INGREDIENTS

- 1/4 teaspoon baking soda
- 1 cup and 1 teaspoon water, divided
- 1 and 1/2 teaspoons vanilla extract
- 1 teaspoon butter, plus more to grease the pan
- 1 cup granulated sugar
- 1 cup firmly packed brown sugar
- 1/2 cup light corn syrup
- 2 and 1/4 cups (about 13 ounces) Spanish peanuts

YIELD: ABOUT 50 PIECES

Recommendation: A candy thermometer is helpful for this recipe, but not necessary.

PEANUT BUTTER COOKIES

INGREDIENTS

- 1 cup granulated sugar, plus more for sprinkling
- 1 cup firmly packed brown sugar
- 1 cup peanut butter
- 1 cup shortening
- 2 eggs, beaten lightly
- 2 and 1/2 cups all-purpose flour
- 2 teaspoons baking soda

METHOD

1. Preheat oven to 350 degrees. Line a baking sheet with parchment paper. Set aside.
2. In a large bowl, beat together both sugars, peanut butter, and shortening until the mixture is smooth and creamy.
3. Mix in eggs, then sift together the flour and baking soda, and add to the mixture until well combined.
4. Roll the dough into walnut-sized balls. Set on the prepared baking sheet.
5. Create a criss-cross design by pressing down on the dough balls with a wet fork.
6. Bake for 10 to 12 minutes.
7. Sprinkle with granulated sugar on top. Let cool on the counter.
8. Store in an airtight container.

YIELD: JUST OVER 2 DOZEN

PEANUT CLUSTERS

INGREDIENTS

- 1 pound white chocolate almond bark (also called vanilla candy coating), broken up
- 6 cups (three 12-ounce bags) semi-sweet chocolate morsels
- 20-ounces dry roasted peanuts

METHOD

1. Line 3 large baking sheets with parchment paper.
2. In a large microwave-safe bowl, heat and stir the almond bark in 20 to 30-second bursts in the microwave until melted, smooth, and piping hot.
3. Stir in the chocolate morsels until they are melted and completely combined with the almond bark.
4. Stir in the peanuts.
5. Drop clusters on the prepared baking sheets by the spoonful. Freeze for 15 minutes.
6. Place in plastic zipper bags to store in the freezer.

YIELD: 2 TO 3 DOZEN

PECANETTES

RECIPE FROM MILLIE ROCHE

METHOD

1. Grease and flour a 12-cup muffin pan. Set aside.
2. In a medium bowl, combine the butter and cream cheese with a mixer until smooth and creamy.
3. Sift the flour, powdered sugar, and salt into the cream cheese mixture, slowly stirring them in.
4. Refrigerate the dough for at least 30 minutes.
5. Preheat oven to 325 degrees.
6. In a saucepan, combine filling ingredients on medium-low heat. Set aside.
7. Shape refrigerated dough into 12 walnut-sized rounds and press each into each cup of the prepared pan, forming a shell.
8. Fill the shells with the warm filling mixture, evenly distributing it among each cup, then top each with a pecan half and bake for 25 to 30 minutes.
9. Cool just slightly before removing from the muffin pan. Gently run a butter knife around the edges of each muffin to loosen them before scooping out.

YIELD: 1 DOZEN

INGREDIENTS

DOUGH

- 1/2 block (4-ounces) cream cheese, softened
- 1/2 cup (1 stick) butter, softened
- 1 cup all-purpose flour
- 1/4 cup powdered sugar
- Dash of salt
- 48 pecan halves, for topping

FILLING

- 1 egg
- 3/4 cup firmly packed brown sugar
- 2 tablespoons butter, softened
- 1 teaspoon vanilla extract
- 2/3 cup finely chopped pecan halves

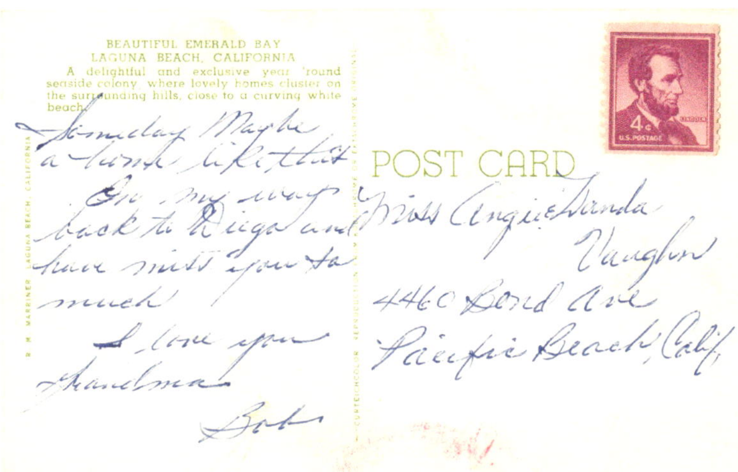

An early postcard from Bob to Wanda and Angie.

PECAN PIE

INGREDIENTS

- 1 unbaked pie crust

CANDIED PECANS

- 1/2 cup granulated sugar
- 1/2 cup firmly packed light brown sugar
- 1 tablespoon ground cinnamon
- 1 teaspoon salt
- 16 ounces pecan halves
- 1 large egg white
- 1/2 teaspoon vanilla extract
- 1 teaspoon water

FILLING

- 1 cup pecans
- 1 cup dark corn syrup
- 2 tablespoons all-purpose flour
- 1 tablespoon butter, melted
- 2 eggs beaten
- 3/4 to 1 cup sugar
- 1 teaspoon vanilla

METHOD

1. Preheat oven to 350 degrees. Prepare the pie crust and set it aside.
2. Prepare candied pecans:
   a. Wet coating: In a large mixing bowl, beat egg white, vanilla, and water until stiff peaks form, which looks like foamy whipped cream. Set aside.
   b. Dry coating: In a separate large bowl, whisk together granulated sugar, brown sugar, cinnamon, and salt.
   c. Add pecans to the egg whites mixture and gently toss to coat. Add the cinnamon sugar mixture and stir gently until the pecans are well coated. Set aside.
3. In a large bowl, stir together filling ingredients. Pour into the unbaked pie shell. Bake for 45 minutes.
4. At 45 minutes, remove the pie from the oven and add the sugar pecan mixture to the top of the pie. Bake for 15 more minutes.
5. Let cool.
6. Store covered on the counter or in the fridge for up to 2 days.

YIELD: 8 TO 10 SLICES

PECAN PIE

PIE CRUST

INGREDIENTS

- 1 cup all-purpose flour
- 1/2 cup shortening
- 1/2 teaspoon salt
- 1/8 to 1/4 cup ice water

METHOD

1. Combine flour, shortening, and salt with a pastry cutter until shortening is in small, manageable chunks. Do not overwork the dough.
2. Slowly add in ice water with one hand while continuing to form the dough into a ball with the other hand. Use as much ice water as needed until the dough comes together nicely into a ball. Do not overwork the dough.
3. Flour your countertop or breadboard. Put the dough on the floured surface and shape it into a ball.
4. Flatten the ball into a disk. Sprinkle flour on top of the dough. Roll out with a rolling pin to the desired size.
5. Line a pie pan with the dough and pinch out the crust.

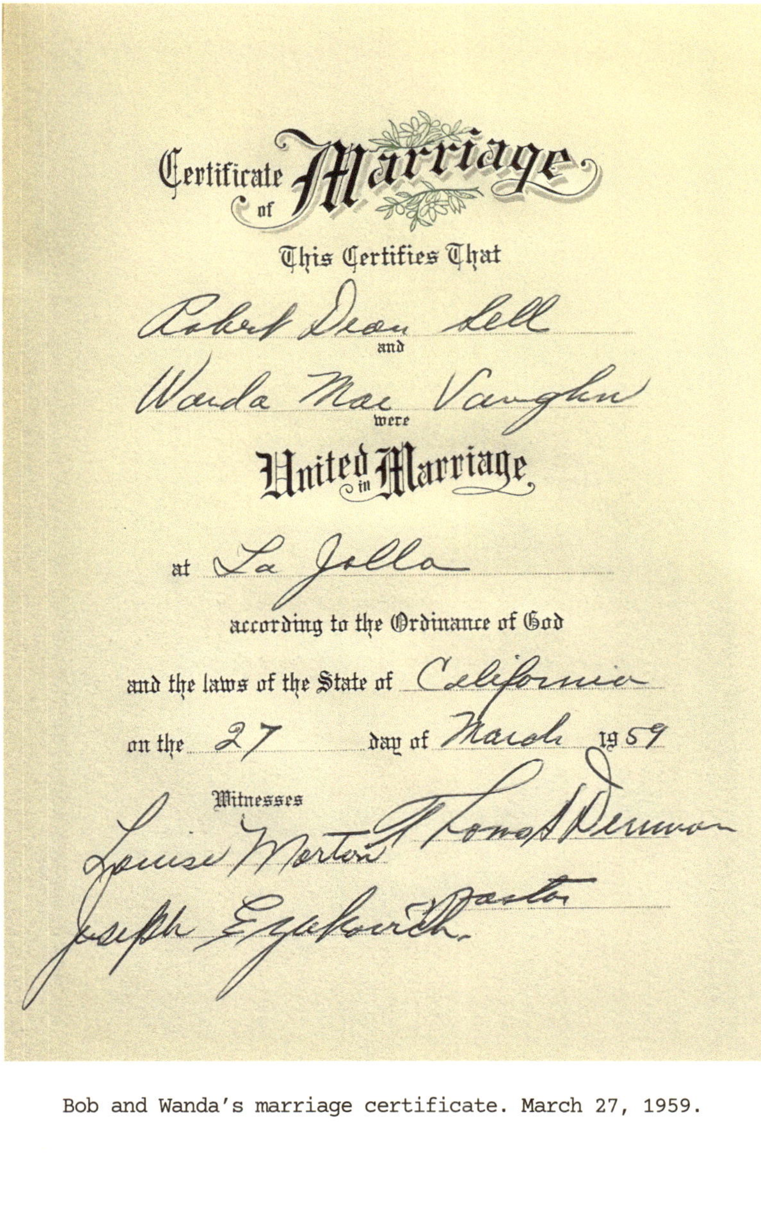

Certificate of Marriage

This Certifies That

Robert Dean Sell

and

Wanda Mae Vaughn

were

United in Marriage

at La Jolla

according to the Ordinance of God

and the laws of the State of California

on the 27 day of March 1959

Witnesses

Louise Morton

Thomas A Denman

[illegible] Pastor

Bob and Wanda's marriage certificate. March 27, 1959.

PISTACHIO CAKE

RECIPE FROM CARLA ZETTER RAEL

METHOD

1. Preheat oven to 350 degrees. Prep a fluted tube pan with nonstick cooking spray. Set aside.
2. Combine all of the cake ingredients except the chopped pistachios in a large bowl. Beat the ingredients together on medium speed with a mixer until well combined.
3. After the batter comes together, gently stir in the chopped pistachios.
4. Pour the batter into the fluted tube pan and bake the cake for about 45 to 50 minutes. You'll know the cake is done when a toothpick or butter knife inserted in the center of the cake comes out clean.
5. Let the cake cool in the pan for about 20 minutes before turning it out onto a cooling rack to cool completely.
6. While the cake is cooling, mix the glaze ingredients in a small bowl and set aside. Once the cake is cool, pour the glaze over the cake. Finish by sprinkling the freshly glazed cake with chopped pistachios.
7. Best served warm.
8. Store covered on the counter or in the fridge.

YIELD: ABOUT 12 TO 14 SLICES

INGREDIENTS

CAKE

- 1 (13.25-ounce) package yellow cake mix
- 1 (3.4-ounce) instant pistachio pudding mix
- 3/4 cup vegetable oil
- 3 large eggs
- 2 teaspoons vanilla extract
- 1/2 cup water
- 3/4 cup sour cream
- 1/2 cup roughly chopped pistachios, plus more for topping

GLAZE

- 1/4 teaspoon vanilla extract
- 1 cup powdered sugar
- 2 tablespoons milk

Bob and Wanda's honeymoon destination, 1959.

POUND CAKE

METHOD

1. Preheat oven to 350 degrees. Spray and flour two loaf pans or one fluted tube pan. Set aside.
2. In a medium bowl, beat egg whites until stiff, which will look light and fluffy, similar to whipped cream, and set aside.
3. Mix the baking soda, sugar, flour, shortening, buttermilk, beaten egg yolks, extract of your choice, and salt in a large bowl until the mixture is well combined, thick, and crumbly.
4. Gently stir in the beaten egg whites last; this makes the batter smooth.
5. Pour/spoon into prepared pan(s) to 3/4 full.
6. Bake for an hour to an hour and ten minutes. You'll know the cake is done when a toothpick or butter knife inserted in the center comes out clean. The top of the cake will have crust-like characteristics.
7. Let the cake completely cool before removing it to a cooling rack.
8. Store covered on the counter or in the fridge.

YIELD: 10 TO 12 SERVINGS

INGREDIENTS

- 6 eggs, separated
- 1/4 teaspoons baking soda
- 3 cups granulated sugar
- 3 cups all-purpose flour
- 1 cup shortening
- 1 cup buttermilk
- 1 teaspoon vanilla, almond, or orange extract
- 1 teaspoon salt

PUMPKIN BREAD

INGREDIENTS

- 2/3 cup shortening
- 2 and 2/3 cups granulated sugar
- 4 eggs
- 1 (15-ounce) can pure pumpkin
- 2/3 cups water
- 3 and 1/3 cup all-purpose flour
- 2 teaspoons baking soda
- 1/2 teaspoon baking powder
- 1 and 1/2 teaspoons salt
- 1 teaspoon ground cloves
- 1 teaspoon cinnamon
- 2/3 cups nuts, chopped, optional

METHOD

1. Preheat oven to 350 degrees. Spray and flour two loaf pans. Set aside.
2. In a large bowl, beat together shortening and sugar until the mixture is smooth and creamy. Mix in eggs, pumpkin, and water.
3. Sift in flour, baking soda, baking powder, salt, and spices. Mix until well combined.
4. Gently stir in nuts if desired.
5. Pour/spoon into the two prepared loaf pans.
6. Bake until a toothpick or butter knife inserted in the center comes out clean, about 60 minutes. Check at 50 minutes and in 10-minute increments after that. If the bread seems done on top but still underbaked in the center, cover it with foil to prevent burning while continuing to bake in 10-minute increments.
7. Wait until cool before inverting onto a cooling rack.
8. To store, place bread in an airtight container or resealable bag at room temperature for up to 4 days. For longer storage, freeze it for up to 2 months. Thaw at room temperature before serving.

YIELD: 2 LOAVES

PUMPKIN PIE

PIE CRUST

INGREDIENTS

- 1 cup all-purpose flour
- 1/2 cup shortening
- 1/2 teaspoon salt
- 1/8 to 1/4 cup ice water

METHOD

1. Combine flour, shortening, and salt with a pastry cutter until shortening is in small, manageable chunks. Do not overwork the dough.
2. Slowly add in ice water with one hand while continuing to form the dough into a ball with the other hand. Use as much ice water as needed until the dough comes together nicely into a ball. Do not overwork the dough.
3. Flour your countertop or breadboard. Put the dough on the floured surface and shape it into a ball.
4. Flatten the ball into a disk. Sprinkle flour on top of the dough. Roll out with a rolling pin to the desired size.
5. Line a pie pan with the dough and pinch out the crust.

METHOD

1. Preheat the oven to 425 degrees.
2. Whisk pure pumpkin, condensed milk, eggs, cinnamon, ginger, nutmeg, and salt in a medium bowl until smooth.
3. Pour mixture into the crust.
4. Bake in the preheated oven for 15 minutes.
5. Reduce oven temperature to 350 degrees and continue baking until a knife inserted 1 inch from the crust comes out clean, about 35 to 40 minutes. Let cool before serving. Serve with whipped topping.
6. Store covered on the counter or in the fridge.

YIELD: 8 TO 10 SERVINGS

INGREDIENTS

- 1 unbaked pie crust
- 1 (15-ounce) can pure pumpkin
- 1 (14-ounce) can sweetened condensed milk
- 2 large eggs
- 1 teaspoon ground cinnamon
- 1 teaspoon ground ginger
- 1/2 teaspoon ground nutmeg
- 1/2 teaspoon salt
- Whipped topping, for serving

PUMPKIN PIE SURPRISE

RECIPE FROM CARLA ZETTER RAEL

INGREDIENTS

- 1 large (29-ounce) can pure pumpkin
- 1 (12-ounce) can evaporated milk
- 1 and 1/2 cup granulated sugar
- 2 teaspoon cinnamon
- 1/2 teaspoon nutmeg
- 1/2 teaspoon salt
- 1/2 teaspoon ground cloves
- 1/2 teaspoon ground ginger
- 1 box yellow cake mix
- 1 cup (2 sticks) butter, melted
- 1 (32-ounce) container heavy cream

METHOD

1. Preheat oven to 350 degrees. Grease a 13x9-inch pan. Set aside.
2. Mix all the ingredients listed, except for the cake mix, butter, and heavy cream.
3. Pour into the prepared pan.
4. Sprinkle the dry yellow cake mix on top.
5. Pour melted butter on top.
6. Bake for 1 hour or until edges are slightly browned.
7. While baking, mix heavy cream with a mixer until it becomes whipped cream. Do not add sugar; the dessert will be sweet enough.
8. Remove from oven, let cool slightly, and serve warm in square slices with a generous dollop of whipped cream on top.

YIELD: 8 TO 10 SERVINGS

RED VELVET CUPCAKES

RECIPE FROM SHANDI SISSERSON

METHOD

1. Preheat oven to 350 degrees. Line two cupcake pans with cupcake liners. Set aside.
2. Sift flour, sugar, baking soda, salt, and baking cocoa in a large bowl. Set aside.
3. In a separate bowl, mix oil, buttermilk, eggs, vinegar, and vanilla extract.
4. Slowly mix in the dry ingredients to the wet ingredients until well blended and a smooth batter is formed. Add red food coloring. Continue to mix until the color is evenly distributed.
5. Divide batter evenly between 24 cupcake liners.
6. Bake for 18 to 22 minutes, rotating pans halfway through. If a toothpick or butter knife does not come out clean, continue baking for additional time, checking every 2 to 3 minutes. Remove from the oven and cool on a cooling rack.
7. While cooling, make the frosting. Mix cream cheese, sugar, and butter until well combined. Mix in vanilla extract. Place in fridge until frosting is slightly stiff, about 30 minutes. Frost when the cupcakes have cooled.
8. Store in an airtight container at room temperature for up to up to 3 days, or in the fridge for up to 5 days.

YIELD: 24 CUPCAKES

INGREDIENTS

- 2 and 1/2 cups all-purpose flour
- 1 and 1/2 cups granulated sugar
- 1 teaspoon baking soda
- 1 teaspoon salt
- 1 heaping tablespoon baking cocoa
- 1 and 1/2 cups vegetable oil
- 1 cup buttermilk, room temperature
- 2 eggs, room temperature
- 1 teaspoon white vinegar
- 2 teaspoons vanilla extract
- 2 tablespoons red food coloring

CREAM CHEESE FROSTING

- 1 pound (two 8-ounce blocks) cream cheese, softened
- 4 cups powdered sugar, sifted
- 1 cup (2 sticks) butter, softened
- 2 teaspoons vanilla extract

SHEATH CAKE

RECIPE FROM LEONA INMON (MEMAW)

METHOD

1. Preheat oven to 350 degrees. Grease a 10x15-inch baking sheet and set aside.
2. Sift flour and sugar together in a large mixing bowl. Set aside.
3. In a saucepan, mix margarine, shortening, baking cocoa, and water. Stir to combine, and bring the mixture to a quick boil. Pour over the flour-sugar mixture and stir well.
4. Add eggs, buttermilk, baking soda, cinnamon, and vanilla extract. Mix well.
5. Pour into the prepared pan and bake for about 20 minutes. You'll know the cake is done when a toothpick or butter knife inserted in the center comes out clean.
6. During the last 5 minutes of baking, start making icing.
    a. Mix margarine, baking cocoa, and milk in a saucepan, and bring to a boil. Stir to combine.
    b. Add powdered sugar, vanilla, cinnamon, and nuts. Stir to combine.
    c. Remove from heat and pour hot icing over hot cake.
7. Allow to cool before serving.
8. Wrap the cake in aluminum foil in the pan to store in the fridge.

YIELD: 18 TO 24 SERVINGS

INGREDIENTS

- 2 cups all-purpose flour
- 2 cups granulated sugar
- 1/2 cup (1 stick) margarine
- 1/2 cup shortening
- 4 tablespoons baking cocoa
- 1 cup water
- 2 eggs, slightly beaten
- 1/2 cup buttermilk
- 1 teaspoon baking soda
- 1 teaspoon cinnamon
- 1 teaspoon vanilla extract

ICING

- 1/2 cup margarine (1 stick)
- 1 tablespoon baking cocoa
- 6 tablespoons milk
- 4 cups powdered sugar
- 1 teaspoon vanilla extract
- 1/2 teaspoon cinnamon
- 1 cup chopped pecans

SHORTBREAD

RECIPE FROM HELEN DOUGLAS

METHOD

1. Preheat oven to 300 degrees. Lightly grease an 11 and 1/2 x 16-inch pan with non-stick cooking spray. Set aside.
2. Mix all ingredients with your hands in a large bowl until the butter is thoroughly incorporated.
3. Press dough into the bottom of the prepared pan.
4. Prick dough all over with a fork.
5. Bake for about 50 to 55 minutes, until slightly brown on top.
6. Remove from the oven, sprinkle with sugar, and cut immediately.
7. Leave the shortbread in the pan until it has cooled.
8. To keep shortbread cookies fresh, store them in an airtight container at room temperature for up to 1 week, or in the fridge for up to 2 weeks.

INGREDIENTS

- 1 pound butter (4 sticks), softened
- 1 cup sugar, plus more for dusting
- 4 cups all-purpose flour, sifted

YIELD: 24 TO 36 BARS, DEPENDING ON THE SIZE CUT

SNICKERDOODLES

METHOD

1. Preheat oven to 350 degrees. Line a baking sheet with parchment paper. Set aside.
2. In a large bowl, mix shortening, 1 and 1/2 cups sugar, and eggs. Sift in flour, cream of tartar, baking soda, and salt.
3. Form dough into balls the size of small walnuts.
4. Combine the cinnamon and the remaining 1/2 cup of sugar, and roll each piece of dough in it.
5. Place rounds on a prepared baking sheet.
6. Bake for 10 minutes.
7. Let cool.
8. Snickerdoodles will keep for up to 1 week in an airtight container at room temperature.

YIELD: 3 DOZEN

INGREDIENTS

- 1 cup shortening
- 2 cups granulated sugar, divided
- 2 eggs
- 2 and 3/4 cups sifted all-purpose flour
- 2 teaspoons cream of tarter
- 1 teaspoon baking soda
- 1/4 teaspoons salt
- 2 teaspoons cinnamon, for dusting

SODA CRACKER TOFFEE

RECIPE FROM TERRISA SELL

INGREDIENTS

- 1 cup firmly packed brown sugar
- 1/2 cup (1 stick) butter or margarine
- 1 sleeve soda crackers
- 1 (12-ounce) package mini chocolate morsels
- 1 cup crushed almonds

METHOD

1. Preheat oven to 350 degrees. Line a baking sheet with parchment paper.
2. Line the prepared baking sheet with a single layer of crackers, tightly packed.
3. Melt brown sugar and butter for 10 minutes in a small saucepan on the stove. Pour over the crackers.
4. Place in the oven for 5 minutes.
5. Top with chocolate morsels and crushed almonds.
6. Refrigerate and let cool.
7. Break toffee into pieces and enjoy!
8. Store in an airtight container on the counter or in the fridge for up to 10 days. Tastes best fresh.

YIELD: ABOUT 3 DOZEN PIECES

STAINED GLASS DESSERT

RECIPE FROM CONNIE BEAM

METHOD

1. Start preparing the day before you plan to serve.
2. In 4 separate bowls, mix 1 cup of boiling water with each package of Jell-O, whisk until well combined and the powder is fully dissolved. Put in the fridge and let them set, which usually takes 2 to 4 hours.
3. Once the Jell-O is set, grease a fluted tube pan and set aside.
4. Cut each flavor of Jell-O into approximately 1/2-inch cubes and mix gently into the fluted tube pan. Set aside in the fridge to keep cool.
5. In a separate bowl, whisk the unflavored gelatin with 1/2 cup cold water until well combined. Add 1 and 1/2 cups of boiling water.
6. Whisk in the condensed milk until well combined. Let cool.
7. Pour completely cooled milk mixture over the Jell-O cubes in the fluted tube pan. Gently stir the Jell-O cubes around until evenly distributed. Cover with plastic wrap and chill in the fridge overnight.
8. When the mold is set, gently run a knife around the edges of the mold. Invert the pan, it should slide right out, cut into servings.
9. Serve cold.
10. Store, covered, in the fridge.

YIELD: ABOUT 12 SERVINGS

INGREDIENTS

- 4 small boxes (3-ounces each) of Jell-O in different flavors/colors
- 5 and 1/2 cups boiling water, divided
- 1 (14-ounce) can sweetened condensed milk
- 3 (1-ounce) packages unflavored gelatin
- 1/2 cup cold water

STRAWBERRY CAKE

METHOD

1. Preheat oven to 350 degrees. Grease and flour two 9-inch cake pans. Set aside.
2. In a large bowl, mix the white cake mix with the Jell-O mix. Add water and oil gradually while mixing. Add eggs one at a time. Stir in the strawberries.
3. Pour batter into the two prepared cake pans.
4. Bake for 25 to 30 minutes until a knife or toothpick inserted in the middle of the cake comes out clean.
5. Let cool in the pans before inverting onto cooling racks.
6. While the cake is baking, make the icing by mixing the butter or margarine and powdered sugar by the cupful until smooth and creamy. Then mix in the milk and salt. Stir in the strawberries. Let set in the fridge until the cake is cool.
7. Let the cake completely cool and the icing sit in the fridge before frosting. Give the icing a stir out of the fridge and cover the top of the first layer. Place the second cake layer on top. Cover the entire outside of the cake. Icing will be a consistency between a traditional icing and a glaze, almost like you could just pour it on the cake.
8. Store in the fridge before serving. Store covered in the fridge for up to 5 days.

YIELD: 8 TO 10 SERVINGS.

INGREDIENTS

- 1 (14.25-ounce) box white cake mix
- 1 (3-ounce) package Strawberry instant Jell-O mix
- 1/2 cup water
- 1/2 cup vegetable oil
- 4 eggs
- 1 cup diced strawberries, washed and hulled

ICING

- 1 cup (2 sticks) butter or margarine, softened
- 4 cups powdered sugar
- 3 tablespoons milk, room temperature
- 1/8 teaspoon salt
- 1 cup diced strawberries, washed, hulled, drained, and dried on a paper towel

SUGAR COOKIES

METHOD

1. In a large bowl, beat together shortening and sugar until the mixture is smooth and creamy.
2. Add the egg and beat till light and fluffy. Add vanilla extract and the remaining ingredients.
3. Cover the dough and chill in the fridge for 30 minutes.
4. Preheat oven to 375 degrees. Line two baking sheets with parchment paper.
5. Divide the dough into walnut-size rounds. Roll each generously in sugar to coat.
6. Place the dough rounds on the prepared baking sheets, spacing them 2 inches apart, and flatten slightly with the bottom of a measuring cup. If needed, peel slowly from the bottom of the measuring cup to lay back on the parchment paper.
7. Bake for 10 minutes.
8. Let them cool completely, then store in an airtight container at room temperature for up to 1 week.

INGREDIENTS

- 2/3 cups shortening
- 3/4 cup granulated sugar, plus more for rolling
- 1 egg
- 1 teaspoon vanilla extract
- 1/2 teaspoon grated orange peel
- 2 cups sifted all-purpose flour
- 1 and 1/2 teaspoons baking powder
- 1/4 teaspoon salt
- 4 tablespoons milk

YIELD: 1 TO 2 DOZEN

SWEDISH PANCAKES

METHOD

1. Preheat oven to 450 degrees. Grease a muffin pan. Set aside.
2. In a large bowl, mix eggs, milk, and flour until smooth. Mix in the remaining ingredients.
3. Spoon the batter into the 12 muffin tins, dividing evenly.
4. Bake for about 10 to 15 minutes.
5. Let cool. Serve warm with jam.
6. Store for up to 3 days in the fridge.

YIELD: 1 DOZEN

Pairs well with: Strawberry Jam (page 210).

INGREDIENTS

- 3 eggs
- 1/2 cup milk
- 1 cup all-purpose flour
- 1/2 teaspoons salt
- 1 tablespoon granulated sugar
- 1/2 teaspoons vanilla extract
- 6 tablespoons butter, softened

SWEDISH SNOWBALLS

METHOD

1. Preheat oven to 325 degrees. Line two baking sheets with parchment paper. Set aside.
2. In a large bowl, beat together the margarine and 1 cup powdered sugar until the mixture is smooth and creamy. Mix in flour and vanilla extract. Fold in nuts.
3. Roll the dough into rounds the size of walnuts. Place on prepared baking sheets.
4. Bake for 30 minutes or more until lightly browned. Flip cookies after 15 minutes to prevent the bottom from over-browning.
5. While warm, roll the cookies in the remaining cup of powdered sugar. If needed, add more powdered sugar when serving.
6. Let cool.
7. Store in an airtight container for up to 1 week. You can freeze both the baked cookies and the unbaked dough. Baked cookies can be frozen for up to 3 months. When thawing, dust with fresh powdered sugar for the best look and taste.

YIELD: ABOUT 5 DOZEN

INGREDIENTS

- 2 cups (4 sticks) margarine, softened
- 2 cups powdered sugar, divided
- 4 cups all-purpose flour
- 3 tablespoons vanilla extract
- 2 cups chopped nuts

TOP SECRET CHOCOLATE FUDGE

METHOD

1. Line a 9x9-inch baking dish with parchment paper. Set aside.
2. Put chocolate morsels and butter in the top bowl of a double boiler and boil for 4 and 1/2 minutes, stirring constantly.
3. While the mixture is still over the double boiler, mix in sugar, eggs, and vanilla extract, stirring constantly.
4. Add in nuts.
5. Using heat-proof gloves, carefully remove the bowl from the double boiler and pour the mixture into the prepared baking dish. Let it set overnight in the fridge.
6. The next day, cut the fudge into serving pieces. Store at room temperature for up to 3 weeks in an airtight container

INGREDIENTS

- 1/2 cup (1 stick) butter
- 1 (12-ounce) package chocolate morsels
- 4 cups powdered sugar
- 2 eggs
- 1 teaspoon vanilla extract
- 1 and 1/2 cups nuts

YIELD: JUST UNDER 2 DOZEN

VANILLA CREAM CHEESE PIE

METHOD

1. Preheat oven to 375 degrees.
2. Mix crust ingredients. Line a pie pan with the crust mixture, patting firmly with the bottom of a measuring cup.
3. Bake the crust in the oven for about 10 minutes.
4. In a large bowl, blend the filling ingredients with a mixer. Pour over the baked crust.
5. Bake for 30 minutes.
6. Refrigerate for 6 to 8 hours or overnight.
7. Cover and store leftover pie in the fridge for up to 5 days.

YIELD: ABOUT 10 SERVINGS

INGREDIENTS

CRUST

- 1 and 1/2 cup graham cracker crumbs
- 1/4 cup granulated sugar
- 1/3 cup butter or margarine, melted

FILLING

- 1 (8-ounce) package cream cheese, softened
- 1 cup sour cream
- 2 eggs, lightly beaten
- 1/2 cup granulated sugar
- 1 and 1/2 teaspoons vanilla extract

WATERGATE SALAD

METHOD

1. In a large bowl, mix the pistachio pudding mix with the can of crushed pineapple in juice.
2. Mix in the whipped topping, marshmallows, and nuts.
3. Pour into a serving bowl and refrigerate for at least 2 hours or up to 24 hours so the marshmallows can soften.
4. Cute served in ice cream sundae cups with chopped pistachios, a few mini marshmallows, a dollop of whipped topping, and a cherry on top.

YIELD: 10 TO 12 SERVINGS

INGREDIENTS

- 1 box (3.4-ounce) pistachio instant pudding mix powder
- 1 large (20-ounce) can crushed pineapple, with juice
- 1 (8-ounce) container whipped topping
- 1 (10-ounce) package mini marshmallows, using more or less as desired
- 1 cup pistachios or almonds, chopped
- Maraschino cherries for topping, optional

ZUCCHINI BREAD

METHOD

1. Preheat oven to 350 degrees. Set aside 1 greased and floured regular-size loaf pan or 2 mini loaf pans.
2. In a large bowl, beat together eggs, sugar, oil, vanilla, and cinnamon until the mixture is smooth and creamy.
3. Mix in flour, baking soda, baking powder, and salt.
4. Gently stir in the zucchini and nuts.
5. Pour into the prepared pans up to 3/4 full and bake for 1 hour.
6. You know the bread is done when a toothpick or butter knife inserted in the middle comes out clean without batter.
7. Zucchini bread can be stored in the fridge in a tightly sealed container for about 1 week. You can also freeze, wrapped tightly, for up to 3 months.

INGREDIENTS

- 3 eggs
- 1 and 1/2 cups granulated sugar
- 1 cup vegetable oil
- 2 teaspoons vanilla extract
- 3 teaspoons cinnamon
- 3 cups all-purpose flour
- 1 teaspoon baking soda
- 1 and 1/4 teaspoons baking powder
- Pinch of salt
- 2 cups grated zucchini
- 1 cup nuts

YIELD: 1 REGULAR LOAF OR 2 MINI LOAVES

Bob and Wanda loved casinos, visiting Vegas, and cruising – if only mostly for the buffets. Wanda had special sequined outfits, from jackets to hats, for these occasions. I think it's only fitting she saved a Pasta Fagioli recipe, seeing as it is among Dean Martin's and Frank Sinatra's favorite foods.

Wanda's Cornbread Dressing is a truly family-famous recipe. Every person who came to Bob and Wanda's for the holidays looked forward to this part of the meal. It is extra special because it calls for her homemade cornbread.

My Aunt Cindy said that Wanda made Corned Beef Cabbage every St. Patrick's Day, a well-known Irish-American tradition. She likely made this to celebrate Bob's Irish heritage, passed down from his mother, Madeline.

Everyone's favorite pork recipe is Aunt Jeanette's Spanish Rice. While creating this book, I had relatives near and far check in to ensure it would be included.

My mom, Alicia, distinctly remembers Frito Pie. Coming home from school, running through the house, yelling "Mom! What's for dinner?!" and Wanda responding "Frito Pie!"

Alicia also remembered that when they lived in Texas, Bob would bring home catfish he had just caught, and Wanda would serve it with big slices of French bread to help catch any small bones that were left in the fish.

My Aunt Angie told me a story about how, after Bob passed away, she and Wanda took a trip back to Texas. One of their first stops was to a restaurant famous for fried catfish and okra. She said it was a bittersweet trip, with a broken heart after having just lost a loved one, and a full heart from sharing time with family and visiting the old Inmon farm.

NOW WE’RE
COOKING

ARTICHOKE AND CRAB DIP

RECIPE FROM TERRISA SELL
AND MIDGE BROWN

HERB CRUST

- 1 cup fine breadcrumbs from French bread
- 1 tablespoon butter, melted
- 2 tablespoons finely chopped parsley
- 1 teaspoon chopped fresh rosemary leaves, or 1/4 teaspoon dried
- 3/4 teaspoon finely chopped fresh basil leaves, or 1/4 teaspoon dried
- 1/4 teaspoon chopped fresh thyme leaves, or 1/8 teaspoon dried
- 1/4 teaspoon chopped fresh oregano leaves, or 1/8 teaspoon dried
- 1/4 teaspoon chopped fresh marjoram leaves, or 1/8 teaspoon dried
- 1 small garlic clove, finely chopped

METHOD

1. Preheat oven to 350 degrees.
2. Mix the herb crust ingredients in a small bowl and set aside.
3. In a large bowl, mix mayonnaise, artichoke hearts, crab meat, cheese, and onion.
4. Spread crab mixture in a 9x9-inch baking dish.
5. Sprinkle with herb crust.
6. Bake uncovered 15 to 20 minutes or until golden brown.
7. Serve with crackers or bread.
8. To store, cool dip to room temperature, transfer to an airtight container, and refrigerate for up to 4 days.

YIELD: ABOUT 20 SERVINGS

INGREDIENTS

- 2 cups mayonnaise
- 1 (12-ounce) jar marinated artichoke hearts, drained and chopped
- 1 (8-ounce) container chopped Dungeness crab meat, canned, lump, or fresh
- 1 cup grated Parmesan cheese
- 1 large onion, very thinly sliced
- Crackers or thin bread slices, for serving

BACON GRAVY

RECIPE FROM THE RUSSELLS

INGREDIENTS

- 4 tablespoons of bacon grease
- 4 tablespoons all-purpose flour
- 2 cups milk
- 1 teaspoon salt
- 1/2 teaspoon black pepper
- 2 to 3 pieces cooked bacon, crumbled

METHOD

1. Put bacon grease in a medium skillet on low heat and add flour to make a roux. Slowly add milk and whisk until it thickens. Keep whisking, or it will cake up.
2. Pour over open-face biscuits.
3. Finish with salt and black pepper. Sprinkle crumbled bacon on top.

YIELD: 4 TO 6 SERVINGS

Pairs well with: Buttermilk Biscuits (page 32).

BAKED BEANS

RECIPE FROM GRANDMA BROWNE

METHOD

1. Preheat oven to 350 degrees.
2. In a medium skillet, fry bacon until cooked through. D
3. Drain, leaving 1 to 2 tablespoons of bacon grease in the pan.
4. Once bacon has slightly cooled, chop into bite-sized bits.
5. Simmer the onion in the remaining bacon grease until soft.
6. Pour the softened onions into a large stockpot with the pork, beans, molasses, brown sugar, and mustard. Stir together.
7. Add the cooked bacon into the pot and stir on low for about 30 minutes.
8. Transfer the mixture to a baking dish and cover with foil. Bake for 30 to 45 minutes. Uncover for the last 5 to 10 minutes.
9. Eat warm or cold as leftovers the next day.

INGREDIENTS

- 1/2 pound bacon
- 1 medium yellow onion, chopped
- 1 (30-ounce) can pork and beans
- 1/2 cup molasses
- 1/2 cup firmly packed brown sugar
- 2 to 3 tablespoons yellow mustard

YIELD: 6 TO 8 SERVINGS

BBQ-STYLE MEAT LOAF

METHOD

1. Preheat oven to 350 degrees. Spray a shallow 7x10 inch loaf pan with nonstick cooking spray. Set aside.
2. Mix beef, breadcrumbs, onion, salt, pepper, 4 to 5 ounces of tomato sauce, water, and beaten egg. Do not overmix.
3. Form into a loaf and put in the loaf pan.
4. Combine the remaining tomato sauce and all other ingredients, and pour over the loaf.
5. Bake for 1 hour and 15 minutes. Check after 1 hour. Baste occasionally. Broil for the last few minutes.
6. Serve hot!
7. To store, refrigerate in an airtight container within 2 hours of cooking.

YIELD: 6 TO 8 SERVINGS

INGREDIENTS

- 1 and 1/2 pounds ground beef
- 1 cup breadcrumbs
- 1 medium onion, finely chopped
- 1 and 1/2 teaspoons salt
- 1/4 teaspoon black pepper
- 2 (8-ounce) or 1 (15-ounce) can tomato sauce, divided
- 1/2 cup water
- 1 egg, beaten
- 3 tablespoons brown sugar
- 3 tablespoons apple cider vinegar
- 2 tablespoons Dijon mustard
- 2 teaspoons Worcestershire sauce

BEEF AND BEER STEW

RECIPE FROM ANGELA VAUGHN

INGREDIENTS

- 1 (32-ounce) container beef broth
- 1 stick (1/2 cup) butter, divided
- 2 and 1/2 pounds beef brisket, cut into 2-inch cubes
- Salt and black pepper, to taste
- 3 medium yellow onions, peeled and quartered
- 4 tablespoons all-purpose flour
- 1 bottle (12 ounces) dark beer
- 3 pounds Yukon Gold potatoes, peeled and quartered
- 1 cup milk

METHOD

1. Pour the beef broth into the slow cooker and set aside.
2. In a large skillet, melt 1 tablespoon butter over medium-high heat. Add the brisket and simmer for 8 minutes. Season with salt and pepper. Transfer meat to the slow cooker, set aside.
3. Add 1 tablespoon butter to the skillet. Add quartered onions and cook over medium heat with a lid over the pan until onions have softened. Transfer to the slow cooker and set aside.
4. Add 2 tablespoons butter to the skillet over medium heat. Add the flour and beer. Bring to a boil, whisking until smooth, making a roux.
5. Pour the roux over the meat and onions in the slow cooker. Gently stir.
6. Cook on low heat in the slow cooker for 6 hours.
7. During the last 30 minutes cooking, place the potatoes in a large pot of salted water, cover and bring to a boil, then simmer for 15 minutes. Drain and return to the pot. Add the remaining 4 tablespoons of butter and mash. Beat in the milk and season with salt and black pepper.
8. Serve warm.
9. To store, refrigerate in an airtight container within 2 hours of cooking.

Yield: 4 to 6 servings

BEEF BRISKET

INGREDIENTS

- 1 (3-pound) beef brisket
- 24-ounces chili sauce
- 1 (1-ounce) envelope dry onion soup mix
- 2 teaspoons garlic powder

METHOD

1. Place beef brisket in a slow cooker.
2. Mix the chili sauce, onion soup mix, and garlic powder and pour over the brisket.
3. Cook on low for 8 to 10 hours.
4. Carefully remove cooked brisket from the slow cooker and place in a serving dish. Slice brisket against the grain; pour gravy over slices.
5. Refrigerate it in an airtight container for up to 4 days or freeze it for up to 2 months.

YIELD: 4 TO 6 SERVINGS

Recommendation: Use a mixture of different types of chili sauces to reach the 24 ounces needed, such as homemade chili sauce (tomato sauce, brown sugar, vinegar, and allspice), chili garlic sauce, and a sweet chili sauce to give it a more complex flavor.

Pairs well with: Nana's Buttermilk Biscuits (page 32) and Bob Jr.'s Coleslaw (page 188) as a beef brisket sandwich with leftovers from the slow cooker.

BROCCOLI SOUP

METHOD

1. Cook chopped broccoli florets in a medium saucepan with chicken broth until tender. Drain and set aside.
2. In a small bowl, mix milk, half and half, and nutmeg. Set aside.
3. In a separate large pan, add butter and onion and cook slowly on low heat until tender. Add flour and cook for 1 to 2 minutes. Slowly add the dairy mixture, and cook until thick. If the mixture is not thickening, add more flour 1 tablespoon at a time. Add cheese, stir well, then add drained cooked broccoli.
4. Puree with a blender. Be careful, as the soup will be hot.
5. Pour into bowls and serve warm.
6. Store in the fridge in an airtight container for up to 4 days.

YIELD: 4 TO 6 SERVINGS

INGREDIENTS

- 2 cups broccoli florets, chopped into small pieces
- 1 (32-ounce) container chicken broth
- 1 cup milk
- 1 (16-ounce) container half and half
- Pinch of nutmeg
- 1 stick (1/2 cup) butter
- 1 small yellow onion, diced fine
- 1/4 cup all-purpose flour, more or less to thicken
- 1 and 1/2 cup grated cheese (mild or sharp cheddar, jack, etc.), plus more for garnish

CHICKEN TORTILLA CASSEROLE

INGREDIENTS

- 1 medium white or yellow onion, chopped
- 2 tablespoons margarine or vegetable oil
- 1 cup chopped jalapeños, seeds removed
- 1 (10.5-ounce) can condensed cream of chicken soup
- 1 (10.5-ounce) can condensed cream of mushroom soup
- Up to 2 cups chicken broth
- 1 (2-pound) rotisserie chicken, skin removed, deboned, and shredded
- 20 to 24 (6-inch) corn and/or flour tortillas, torn into pieces
- 1 pound grated cheddar cheese

METHOD

1. Preheat oven to 350 degrees. Spray a 13x9-inch baking dish with cooking spray. Set aside.
2. In a large saucepan on the stovetop, brown onions in the margarine or oil. Add green jalapeños, condensed cream of chicken, and condensed cream of mushroom soup. Slowly add chicken broth until the mixture begins to boil.
3. Add shredded rotisserie chicken to this mixture, stirring constantly for 2 to 3 minutes. Remove from heat.
4. Alternate layers of torn tortilla pieces, chicken mixture, and cheese in the prepared baking dish until all of the torn tortillas are used up. Usually makes two layers.
5. Bake for 30 minutes until bubbly and golden brown.
6. Serve warm out of the oven.
7. Leftover chicken tortilla casserole can be safely stored in the refrigerator for up to 4 days.

YIELD: 10 TO 12 SERVINGS

Recommendation: Serve with tortilla chips.

Pairs well with: Salsa (page 206) and Salsa Verde (page 207).

CHILI BEEF STIR-FRY

RECIPE FROM SUWARNI HARPER, MIKE SAWYER'S WIFE

INGREDIENTS

- 2 tablespoons chili-garlic sauce
- 2 tablespoons soy sauce
- 2 tablespoons sherry
- 1 teaspoon honey
- 2 teaspoons toasted sesame oil
- 2 teaspoons cornstarch
- 1 pound flank steak, trimmed
- Salt and black pepper, to taste
- 2 tablespoons vegetable oil, divided
- 6 green onions, ends trimmed and thinly sliced, divided
- 4 garlic cloves, minced
- 1 tablespoon grated ginger
- 12 ounces snow peas

METHOD

1. Whisk the chili-garlic sauce, soy sauce, sherry, honey, sesame oil, and cornstarch in a small bowl and set aside.
2. Cut the beef lengthwise along the grain into 3 or 4 (2-inch) wide pieces. Then, slice each piece of beef across the grain into about 1/8-inch thick pieces. Pat the beef dry and season well with salt and black pepper to taste.
3. Heat 1 tablespoon of the oil in a medium skillet over high heat until smoking. Add the beef and cook, stirring occasionally, until well browned, about 4 to 5 minutes. Remove to a plate.
4. Return the skillet to the stove over medium-low heat. Add the remaining 1 tablespoon of oil, half of the green onions, the garlic, and the ginger, and cook until just fragrant and brightening in color, about 30 seconds.
5. Stir in the snow peas, and cook, stirring occasionally, until bright green, about 2 minutes. Whisk in the chili-garlic sauce mixture. Remove the pan from the heat, and add the beef back in with the accumulated juices.
6. Toss to coat and transfer to a serving platter. Serve immediately with rice, and sprinkle the dish with the remaining green onions.

YIELD: 2 TO 4 SERVINGS

Recommendation: Pairs well with a glass of Moscato d'Asti.

Wanda dancing on her honeymoon with Bob in 1959.

CORNBREAD DRESSING

METHOD

1. Prepare Wanda's Southern Cornbread recipe (page 147).
2. Preheat oven to 400 degrees. Spray a 3-quart glass baking dish with non-stick spray.
3. Crumble prepared cornbread from Wanda's Southern Cornbread recipe and toss together with white bread in the baking dish. Set aside.
4. Prepare giblet broth (page 147). Set aside.
5. In a large pan, fry onions and celery in margarine, cooking and stirring until tender but not brown. Let cool.
6. Add sage, salt, and black pepper to taste. Toss to coat.
7. Add mushroom soup and evaporated milk to the above. Add giblets.
8. Pour over bread and toss well.
9. Pour about 3 cups of broth from the giblets over the mixture until the broth rises to the top slightly.
10. Mix in chopped-up hard-boiled eggs.
11. Bake for 45 minutes to an hour, until set.
12. Serve warm.

YIELD: 10 TO 12 SERVINGS

INGREDIENTS

- 2 cups prepared cornbread
- 6 slices white bread, torn into small pieces
- 2 cups chopped yellow or white onions
- 2 cups chopped celery
- 1/2 cup (1 stick) margarine
- 6 teaspoons dried sage leaves
- Salt and black pepper, to taste
- 1 (10.5-ounce) can condensed cream of mushroom soup
- 1 small (5-ounce) can evaporated milk
- Turkey giblets or gizzards
- Broth from turkey giblets or gizzards
- 3 hard-boiled eggs, chopped-up

CORNBREAD DRESSING

WANDA'S SOUTHERN CORNBREAD

INGREDIENTS

- 1 cup buttermilk
- 1 cup cornmeal
- 1 egg
- 1/4 teaspoon baking powder
- 1/4 teaspoon salt

METHOD

1. The night before, soak the cornmeal in buttermilk in the fridge. The finer the cornmeal, the less grainy the bread will be.
2. Preheat oven to 400 degrees. Grease and flour a cast-iron pan.
3. In a medium bowl, mix the remaining ingredients with the soaked cornmeal.
4. Pour batter into the prepared pan.
5. Bake until firm and a toothpick or butter knife comes out clean, about 15 to 20 minutes.

GIBLET BROTH

INGREDIENTS

- Giblets from 1 turkey or 1 pound gizzards
- 1 teaspoon dried thyme leaves
- 1/2 teaspoon dried sage leaves
- 1 medium onion, quartered
- 2 celery stalks, quartered
- 4 cups (32 ounces) chicken broth

METHOD

1. Add all broth ingredients into a 2-quart saucepan.
2. Bring to a boil and then reduce the heat to low and simmer, covered, for at least 1 hour.
3. Strain out solids, separate out giblets, and set them aside. Set aside the strained broth.

Bob on his honeymoon with Wanda in 1959.

CORNED BEEF CABBAGE

METHOD

1. Prepare Spice Mix (page 151), Meat Brine (page 151), and start brining the meat 5 to 7 days before the day you plan to serve.
2. On the day you are making the dish, Place the rinsed beef in a stockpot and cover with water. Add remainder of Spice Mix, cover, and bring to a boil.
3. Reduce heat and simmer until the beef is just about fork-tender, about 2 hours.
4. While the beef is simmering, cut the potatoes in half. Peel the carrots and cut them into 3-inch pieces. Cut the cabbage into small wedges.
5. Add potatoes and carrots once the beef has cooked for 2 hours. Put the lid back on and cook until vegetables are almost tender, about 10 minutes.
6. Add cabbage and cook until tender, about 15 more minutes.
7. Remove the meat and let it rest for 15 minutes. Leave the broth and vegetables in the pot.
8. Slice meat against the grain.
9. Serve warm with the vegetables and broth.
10. To store, place leftovers within two hours of cooking in an airtight container in the fridge for 3 to 4 days. For longer storage, freeze for up to 2 to 3 months.

INGREDIENTS

- 1 (3-pound) flat cut beef brisket, brined
- Spice Mix (page 151)
- 10 small red potatoes (or a mixture of red and Yukon Gold potatoes)
- 5 medium carrots
- 1 large head of cabbage

YIELD: 6 TO 8 SERVINGS

CORNED BEEF CABBAGE

SPICE MIX

INGREDIENTS

- 1/2 tablespoon anise seeds
- 1/2 tablespoon mustard seeds
- 1/2 tablespoon whole black peppercorns
- 1 teaspoon whole cloves
- 4 whole cardamom pods
- 3 large bay leaves
- 1/2 tablespoon ground coriander
- 1/2 tablespoon red pepper flakes
- 1 teaspoon ground ginger

METHOD

1. In a small pot, toast the anise seeds, mustard seeds, black peppercorns, cloves, and cardamom pods until fragrant, about 2 to 3 minutes.
2. Remove from heat. In a spice grinder, pulse the toasted mixture with the bay leaves.
3. In a small bowl, mix pulsed spices with the remaining seasonings. Set aside.

MEAT BRINE

INGREDIENTS

- 8 cups water
- 1/3 cup salt
- 2 and 1/2 teaspoons pink curing salt
- 1 and 1/2 tablespoons Spice Mix
- 1/3 cup brown sugar, firmly packed
- 1/2 stick cinnamon

METHOD

1. Start brining process 5 to 7 days prior to serving.
2. Place all ingredients in a stock pot and bring to a boil.
3. Remove from heat and let cool. Once cool, refrigerate until chilled.
4. Place the beef in the chilled mixture. If the meat floats, you may need to weight it down with a plate or bowl. Leave in fridge for 5 to 7 days.
5. The day you are ready to make the dish, thoroughly rinse the brined meat before cooking.

Bob and Wanda on their honeymoon at Big Bear Lake, California, in 1959.

FRIED OKRA

METHOD

1. Slice okra into 1/4- to 1/2-inch pieces.
2. Place the okra in a bowl and wash with water. Drain the bowl, leaving the okra wet. Set aside.
3. Mix cornmeal, salt, black pepper, and flour in a large bowl.
4. Pour the buttermilk in a separate small bowl and dip the okra in the buttermilk, then place it in a strainer.
5. Pour the strained okra into the cornmeal mixture and toss until all of the okra is covered. Set aside.
6. Melt shortening and bacon grease in a skillet on medium to medium-high heat. The oil should not be so deep that it fully covers the okra.
7. When the oil is hot (add one piece of okra and see if it sizzles), add a few pieces of okra and cook, stirring frequently, until brown and crisp.
8. Fry okra in batches so as not to overcrowd the pan.
9. Remove okra from the skillet and place on paper towels to drain.
10. Add additional shortening and bacon grease as needed, but be sure you heat it before adding more okra.
11. Serve warm.

INGREDIENTS

- 6 to 8 ounces fresh okra
- 1 cup corn meal
- Salt and black pepper, to taste
- 1/4 cup all-purpose flour
- 1 cup buttermilk
- 1/2 cup shortening
- 4 tablespoons bacon grease

YIELD: ABOUT 4 SERVINGS

Variation: Fry with the shortening and olive oil for a vegetarian version.

FRIED SPAM

METHOD

1. Cut the Spam lengthwise into 8 equal slices.
2. In a large skillet over medium-high heat, cook Spam slices for 3 to 5 minutes or until caramelized, flipping halfway through; remove Spam from skillet and set aside.
3. In the same pan, cook soy sauce, brown sugar, and sriracha until smooth.
4. Put Spam in the sauce and cook for 2 more minutes or until the slices are fully coated.
5. Serve immediately.

INGREDIENTS

- 1 (12-ounce) container of Spam
- Soy sauce, to taste
- Brown sugar, to taste
- Sriracha (or your favorite hot sauce), to taste

YIELD: 8 SLICES

Pairs well with: Deviled eggs recipe (page 190) for Spam Deviled Eggs.

FRITO PIE

RECIPE FROM ALICIA SELL

METHOD

1. Preheat oven to 350 degrees.
2. Warm the chili in a large saucepan over medium heat on the stove.
3. First layer: Spread a layer of Fritos, approximately 1/3 of the package, along the bottom of a 12-inch skillet or a 13x9-inch baking dish. Spoon half of the chili evenly over the Fritos, then spread one can of diced tomatoes over the chili.
4. Second Layer: Add another layer of Fritos, about 1/3 of the package, and then sprinkle half the shredded cheese evenly over them. Spoon the remaining chili evenly over everything.
5. Third Layer: Add one final layer of Fritos, spread the second can of diced tomatoes evenly over the Fritos, and sprinkle the remaining cheese evenly over everything with the onions.
6. Place the baking dish onto a foil-covered baking sheet (to prevent overflow drippings) and bake on the middle rack of the oven for 25 to 30 minutes or until the cheese is melted and bubbly. Allow the Frito pie to cool for a few minutes before serving. Add desired toppings.

INGREDIENTS

- 15 ounces Frito scoops
- 2 (14-ounce) cans of chili
- 2 (10-ounce) cans diced tomatoes and green chilies, drained (such as Ro-Tel)
- 3 cups shredded sharp cheddar cheese
- 3/4 cups diced white onions (about 1/2 a large onion)

YIELD: ABOUT 8 SERVINGS

Recommendation: Additional toppings at the discretion of the family, such as lettuce, sour cream, corn, green onion, more diced tomatoes, etc.

GUMBO

RECIPE FROM JOY (SHAM) SHAMBURGER

INGREDIENTS

- 1/2 tablespoon avocado oil
- 1 and 1/2 pounds boneless skinless chicken thighs, diced
- Salt and black pepper, to taste
- 12 ounces smoked andouille sausage, sliced
- 1/2 cup butter, diced
- 1/2 cup all-purpose flour
- 1 cup green bell pepper, finely diced
- 1 cup red bell pepper, finely diced
- 1 cup orange bell pepper, finely diced
- 1 cup yellow onion, finely diced
- 1 cup celery, finely diced
- 6 large cloves of garlic, minced
- 1 tablespoon Cajun spice blend (paprika, salt, garlic powder, black pepper, white pepper, onion powder, dried oregano, cayenne, and thyme)
- 1 tablespoon tomato paste
- 2 cups sliced fresh okra
- 1 (14.5-ounce) canned diced tomatoes
- 3 dried bay leaves
- 6 sprigs fresh thyme
- 4 cups chicken broth
- 1 tablespoon coconut aminos
- 1 teaspoon hot sauce
- To thicken, if needed: 1/4 cup all-purpose flour and 3/4 cup water
- Salt, to taste
- 1 pound peeled and deveined shrimp
- Sliced green onion, for serving

Recommendation: Serve with prepared white rice.

Variation: Use gluten-free all-purpose flour for a non-gluten version.

GUMBO

METHOD

1. Heat a large stockpot over medium heat. Add in avocado oil. Add the chicken thighs to the pot and season with salt and black pepper. Cook the chicken until mostly brown, then add the smoked sausage. Let the meat continue to cook until the chicken is fully cooked. Transfer the chicken, sausage, and any remaining liquid from the pot to a bowl, then set it aside.
2. Next, make the roux. Add the diced butter to the pot and let it melt over medium heat. Whisk in the flour once the butter is melted to create a thick paste. Let the flour and butter mixture cook over medium heat, whisking frequently, for around 20 minutes until it becomes a dark, rich color. Be careful to watch the roux so it does not burn.
3. Add the bell peppers, onion, celery, garlic, Cajun spice blend, and tomato paste to the hot roux and allow the veggies to cook for a few minutes until they become tender.
4. Add the okra, diced tomatoes, herbs, chicken broth, coconut aminos, hot sauce, and cooked chicken and sausage back to the pot. Stir until well combined and then bring to a boil. Once boiling, reduce the heat to a simmer, cover, and let the gumbo simmer for an hour.
5. If needed, create a slurry to thicken the gumbo by whisking together 1/4 cup of all-purpose flour with 3/4 cup of water until a slurry forms. Be sure to whisk the slurry mixture well to avoid lumps. Stir the slurry mixture into the gumbo a little at a time, allowing it to cook for a few more minutes until it thickens. Add more salt, to taste, at this point if needed.
6. Lastly, stir in the shrimp and cook for a few more minutes until done. Be sure not to leave for too long and overcook the shrimp.
7. Once the shrimp is done, serve the gumbo warm over prepared white rice.
8. Store, covered, in the fridge for up to three days.

YIELD: 8 TO 10 SERVINGS

GINGER TOMATO HALIBUT

METHOD

1. Preheat a medium to large skillet, add oil.
2. Add fillets to oil, cover and cook for about 5 minutes on each side until lightly browned, and fish can be flaked with a fork. Remove to a warmed serving plate.
3. Heat the butter in the same skillet over medium heat. Add the ginger. Cook and stir until fragrant, about 2 minutes. Stir in the garlic, cilantro, tomato, and salt to taste.
4. Pour hot ginger-tomato sauce over the halibut. Squeeze a lemon over the dish. Dress with fresh cilantro.
5. Serve with rice.

YIELD: 4 SERVINGS

Variation: Make with lingcod or sea bass instead of halibut.

INGREDIENTS

- 4 (6-ounce) halibut fillets, patted dry
- 2 tablespoons olive oil
- 2 tablespoons butter
- 1 tablespoon fresh ginger, minced
- 3 cloves garlic, minced
- 2 tablespoons fresh cilantro, plus more for dressing
- 1 tomato, diced
- Salt, to taste
- Squeeze of lemon
- Cooked white rice

MR. AND MRS. L. D. INMON

OBSERVE GOLDEN WEDDING—Mr. and Mrs. L. D. Inmon, Rt. 4, Hillsboro were honored Sunday, Dec. 22, on their 50th wedding anniversary with a reception at the Hillsboro State Bank Community Room. The occasion was from 2 to 5 in the afternoon. Mr. and Mrs. Inmon were married Dec. 20, 1913 at Menlow by Brother J. T. Strickland. They both have resided in Hill County for over 65 years and are members of the Whitney Church of Christ. The Inmons have five living children: Weldon Inmon, Mrs. H. Chastain and Mrs. John McRae, all of Dallas, Mrs. Robert Sell of Los Angeles, Calif., and Mrs. F. W. Sawyers of Waco. They also have 18 grandchildren and 12 great grandchildren.

Wanda's parents, Loyf and Leona Inmon, known as Pawpaw and Memaw. 1963 Golden wedding 50th anniversary announcement in the local paper.

LASAGNA ROLL-UPS

RECIPE FROM IRENE URTON

METHOD

1. Preheat oven to 375 degrees. Grease a 13x9-inch baking dish. Set aside.
2. In a large skillet, brown the meat with garlic and seasoning. Once browned, stir in pasta sauce, diced tomatoes, and 1/2 cup of the Parmesan cheese. Let simmer on low.
3. In a medium bowl, mix eggs, milk, cream cheese, and shredded Italiano or Mexican cheese until smooth and creamy. Set aside.
4. Cook 12 to 16 lasagna noodles following package instructions in a large pot. Drain and let the noodles cool slightly.
5. Pour or spoon half of the meat mixture into the bottom of the prepared baking dish.
6. Flatten out cooked noodles, about 4 at a time, side by side, and spread the cream cheese mixture evenly on the noodles. Roll up noodles and place in the baking dish on the meat mixture. Continue in this fashion until all lasagna noodles have the cream cheese mixture spread and are rolled in the baking dish on top of the meat layer.
7. Spoon or pour the remainder of the meat mixture on top of the lasagna. Sprinkle the remaining 1/2 cup of Parmesan cheese on top.
8. Cover the baking dish. Cook for 45 to 50 minutes, uncovering the dish for the last 5 minutes.
9. Serve warm.
10. Store, covered in the fridge for up to 3 days or in the freezer for up to 2 months.

Yield: 10 to 12 servings

INGREDIENTS

- 1 pound ground beef
- 4 cloves garlic, minced
- 2 teaspoons seasoning salt of your choice (salt, black pepper, garlic powder, crushed red pepper flakes, thyme)
- 1 (24-ounce) jar tomato and basil pasta sauce
- 7 ounces (1/2 of a 14-ounce can) petite diced tomatoes
- 1 cup shredded Parmesan cheese, divided
- 2 eggs
- 2 tablespoons milk
- 1 cup (1 block) cream cheese, softened
- 1 cup shredded Italiano or Mexican cheese
- 12 to 16 lasagna noodles

MEATBALLS

METHOD

1. In a large bowl, mix everything except oil with the meat.
2. Shape into meatballs.
3. Brown in a skillet with vegetable oil in batches of 10 or so; don't overcrowd the pan. You will need to periodically cover the meatballs with a lid so they cook all the way through.
4. Set cooked meatballs aside and cover with aluminum foil; they will continue to cook slightly.
5. Serve with spaghetti noodles and sauce immediately, or let cool completely and freeze for later.

YIELD: ABOUT 40 GOOD-SIZED MEATBALLS

INGREDIENTS

- 3 pounds ground beef
- 2 eggs
- 1 cup grated Parmesan cheese
- 2 teaspoons dried parsley flakes
- 4 tablespoons finely chopped onions
- 2 cloves garlic, crushed
- 2 teaspoons salt
- 1/2 cup breadcrumbs
- 1 teaspoon crushed dried sweet basil
- 1 teaspoon oregano leaf
- 1/4 teaspoon black pepper
- 6 tablespoons vegetable oil

PASTA FAGIOLI

METHOD

1. Make the morning you plan to serve.
2. In a skillet, add the vegetable oil and brown the beef and garlic until most of the meat's moisture has evaporated. Add all ingredients except the pasta to a slow cooker. The slow cooker will be very full.
3. Cook on low for 7 to 8 hours. Stirring occasionally.
4. Add uncooked pasta for the last 30 minutes.
5. Season with salt and black pepper, to taste, and serve warm.
6. Store covered in the fridge for up to 5 days. Overnight, it will thicken to a more pasta-like or chili-like consistency.

YIELD: 10 TO 12 SERVINGS

INGREDIENTS

- 2 pounds ground beef
- 4 to 6 garlic cloves, minced
- 2 tablespoons vegetable oil
- 1 yellow onion, chopped
- 3 carrots, diced
- 2 (15-ounce) cans diced tomatoes, with juice
- 1 (15-ounce) can kidney beans, drained
- 1 (15-ounce) can white beans, drained
- 2 (14-ounce) containers of beef stock
- 4 stalks celery, diced
- 5 tablespoons dried parsley
- 2 teaspoons black pepper
- 1 teaspoon Tabasco sauce
- 1 (20-ounce) jar spaghetti sauce
- Salt and black pepper
- 8 ounces (2 cups) ditalini pasta noodles, uncooked

POTATO CHIP FRIED CHICKEN TENDERS

RECIPE FROM GREG SISSERSON

INGREDIENTS

- 4 whole chicken breasts, de-boned, skinned, halved, and cut into 1 to 2-inch strips

MARINADE

- 1 quart buttermilk
- 2 tablespoons hot sauce
- 1 and 1/2 teaspoon chili powder
- 1 teaspoon paprika
- 1/2 teaspoon garlic powder
- 1 teaspoon salt
- 1 teaspoon black pepper

BREADING

- 2 cups Sweet Maui Onion potato chips, crushed
- 1 cup all-purpose flour
- 1 and 1/2 teaspoon chili powder
- 1 teaspoon paprika
- 1/2 teaspoon garlic powder
- 1 teaspoon salt
- 1 teaspoon black pepper

EGG WASH

- 2 eggs
- 1 tablespoon water

FOR FRYING

- 1/2 cup (1 stick) butter

METHOD

1. In a large resealable bag, soak the prepared chicken breasts in the buttermilk marinade overnight.
2. Place the crushed potato chips in a large resealable bag. Add flour, chili powder, paprika, garlic powder, salt, and black pepper and shake together to combine. Pour the dry mixture onto a baking sheet and set aside.
3. Combine eggs and water in a separate large resealable bag. Shake together until well mixed.
4. Put all of the marinated chicken strips in the egg mixture and shake the bag, coating each of the pieces.
5. Dredge each piece of chicken through the dry ingredient mixture until each piece is well coated. Set aside.
6. Melt 1/2 cup butter in a large skillet over low-medium heat.
7. Add chicken and cook on each side until golden brown. Cook until the chicken is no longer pink in the middle. Cook in batches, not to overcrowd the pan. You may need to clear the pan of leftover flour mixture and rebutter the skillet halfway through.
8. Drain chicken on paper towels. Keep warm in a low-temperature oven or on a plate under aluminum foil.

YIELD: ABOUT 8 SERVINGS.

Pairs well with: Baked Beans (page 138), Coleslaw (page 188), and Buttermilk Biscuits (page 32) for a fried chicken sandwich and baked beans on the side.

POZOLE

RECIPE FROM CARLA ZETTER RAEL

METHOD

1. In a large pan, cook diced chicken, onions, and garlic in oil until browned. Add garlic salt, onion powder, salt, cumin, and chili powder when the meat is almost browned.
2. In a separate pot, add chicken broth and bring to a simmer. Add browned and seasoned meat and onions to the broth and cook on a low simmer for 20 to 30 minutes until the chicken is tender.
3. Add hominy last. Bring back to a low simmer, then remove from the heat.
4. Serve warm with your choice of toppings.
5. Store covered in the fridge for up to 5 days or in the freezer for 2 months.

YIELD: 6 TO 8 SERVINGS.

Recommendation: Garnish with chopped cilantro, radishes, pico de gallo, and tortilla chips.

INGREDIENTS

- 2 to 4 tablespoons vegetable oil
- 1 and 1/2 pounds boneless skinless chicken thighs, diced
- 1 large yellow or white onion, chopped
- 2 cloves garlic, minced
- 1/4 teaspoon garlic salt
- 1/4 teaspoon onion powder
- 1/4 teaspoon salt
- 1/4 teaspoon cumin
- 1/4 teaspoon chili powder
- 2 (32-ounce) containers chicken broth
- 1 large (25-ounce) can of hominy, drained

QUESABIRRIA TACOS

RECIPE FROM SHANDI SISSERSON

METHOD

1. Start making the morning of.
2. In batches, brown each side of the chuck roast and short ribs in a medium skillet with oil.
3. Add onion, garlic, carrots, bay leaves, and dried peppers to a slow cooker. Cover with chicken broth. Add chili powder, oregano, cumin, salt, and paprika. Stir to combine. Add in meat.
4. Cook on low for 8 to 10 hours.
5. Once the meat is cooked, remove it from the broth and shred. Set aside.
6. To make quesabirria tacos, heat a large skillet over medium heat.
7. Remove some of the broth and pour it into a small shallow bowl big enough to allow a tortilla to be dipped into. Dip the corn tortilla into the broth in the shallow bowl.
8. Place dipped tortilla in the heated skillet, top with the chopped meat and cheese. Fold the taco over and press down with a spatula to form a quesadilla. Cook until the taco is crisp and golden on the bottom, about 2 to 3 minutes. Flip and continue cooking the other side.
9. Remove from heat and allow to cool briefly before serving.
10. Serve with a bowl of the broth to dip the tacos in.

YIELD: 3 TO 4 SERVINGS

Recommendation: Garnish with fresh cilantro and diced white onion

INGREDIENTS

- 2 pounds chuck roast, cut into 2 large chunks
- 1 pound short ribs, bone in
- 2 tablespoons vegetable oil
- 1 large yellow onion, cut in half
- 1 garlic bulb
- 1 carrot, cut into 4 pieces
- 5 bay leaves
- 8 guajillo chiles, stems and seeds removed
- 7 to 8 cups chicken broth
- 2 and 1/2 teaspoons chili powder
- 1 teaspoon oregano
- 1 teaspoon ground cumin
- 1 teaspoon salt
- 1/2 teaspoon paprika
- 1 package (30-count) white corn tortillas
- Oaxacan, Mozzarella, Monterey Jack cheese, or a Mexican cheese blend

SEVEN-LAYER SALAD

METHOD

In a very large serving bowl, layer the following ingredients:

Layer 1: Chopped iceberg lettuce
Layer 2: Chopped celery
Layer 3: Chopped onions
Layer 4: Chopped water chestnuts
Layer 5: Frozen petite green peas topped with mayonnaise
Layer 6: Grated cheese
Layer 7: Sliced hard-boiled eggs and chopped green peppers (if using)
Garnish with cooked bacon bits.

YIELD: 8 TO 12 SERVINGS

Variations: Add more layers if you like. For a little color, add diced tomatoes to the top along with the bacon bits.

INGREDIENTS

- 1 large head iceberg lettuce, rinsed, dried, and chopped
- 3 to 4 stalks of celery, chopped
- 1 medium red onion, chopped
- 1 (8-ounce) can water chestnuts, drained and chopped
- 1 (10-ounce) package frozen petite green peas
- 1 and 1/4 cup mayonnaise
- 10 ounces grated cheese, Mexican or light cheddar
- 4 hard boiled eggs, peeled and sliced
- 1 pound bacon, cooked and chopped
- 1 cup green peppers, chopped, optional
- 1 tomato, chopped, optional

SOUTHERN FRIED CATFISH

RECIPE FROM ANGELA VAUGHN

METHOD

1. Combine cornmeal, seasoning salt, black pepper, and garlic powder in a shallow dish. Set aside.
2. Pour milk into a separate shallow dish. Set aside.
3. Pat the fish dry with paper towels. If your fillets are long, cut them in half for a better frying experience.
4. Heat oil and butter in a large skillet over medium heat.
5. Dip a catfish fillet in the milk, and shake off any excess. Transfer milk-soaked fish to the cornmeal mixture and gently roll to coat on both sides. Repeat with all fillets.
6. Place the fish in the hot skillet and cook until golden brown on each side (about 5 to 7 minutes per side). When it's done, the fish will flake easily with a fork. It is recommended to cook the fish in batches to avoid overcrowding the pan.
7. Drain fish on paper towels.
8. Serve warm.

INGREDIENTS

- 1 cup yellow cornmeal
- 1 to 2 tablespoons seasoning salt (salt, black pepper, garlic powder, crushed red pepper flakes, thyme)
- 1 cup milk or buttermilk
- 4 catfish fillets, about 3 to 4 ounces each
- 3 tablespoons vegetable oil
- 3 tablespoons salted butter
- 1/4 teaspoon garlic powder
- 1/4 teaspoon ground black pepper

YIELD: 4 SERVINGS

Recommendation: Garnish with lemon wedges and fresh parsley.

SPANISH RICE

RECIPE FROM JEANETTE HARSH

METHOD

1. Preheat oven to 350 degrees.
2. Cut off the stem to peel tomatoes and make a criss-cross x on the bottom. Put the tomatoes in boiling water for 60 seconds, then submerge them in ice-cold water. The tomato skin will peel right off. Dice tomatoes.
3. Cut the fat off the pork chops and dice the meat into bite-sized pieces.
4. In a large skillet on medium-high heat, add olive oil. Cook the meat while stirring. After about 5 to 7 minutes, add the chopped green pepper and garlic.
5. While cooking, lower the heat to medium-low. Add diced tomatoes.
6. While everything is simmering, add rice and water. Cover the pan, and let it cook slowly on low for 10 to 15 minutes.
7. Then, pour the entire dish into a large casserole and bake it covered in the oven until the rice is cooked and the water is absorbed, about 45 minutes.
8. Remove the cover and continue to cook for about 15 minutes.
9. Serve hot, season with salt and black pepper to taste. Top with cheese if you'd like.

INGREDIENTS

- 3 to 5 tomatoes, peeled and diced
- 6 large pork chops
- 3 tablespoons olive oil
- 1 to 2 green peppers, chopped
- 5 to 6 cloves garlic, chopped
- 1 cup uncooked rice (equals 3 cups cooked)
- 1 cup water
- Salt and black pepper, to taste
- Grated cheese, optional

YIELDS: 6 TO 8 SERVINGS

Variations: Add more tomatoes and garlic to the recipe for a stronger flavor. Mix in corn, red pepper, white onion, paprika, jalapeño, or fried egg.

STEAK STROGANOFF

METHOD

1. Start to make the morning of.
2. Place the steak in the bottom of a slow cooker, and season with salt and pepper to taste. Place the onion on top of the beef, then add the mushroom soup, mushrooms, and water. Season by pouring the white wine, chives, garlic, Worcestershire sauce, and bouillon on top.
3. Cover and cook on low for 6 to 7 hours. Stir in the sour cream, flour, and parsley, then continue cooking for an additional 1 hour.
4. During the last few minutes of cooking, fill a large pot with lightly salted water and bring it to a rapid boil. Boil egg noodles for 7 to 9 minutes. Drain.
5. Serve the stroganoff over the egg noodles.
6. Store leftover beef stroganoff in an airtight container in the fridge for up to 4 days. Reheat in the microwave or on the stove.

YIELD: 6 SERVINGS

INGREDIENTS

- 1 and 1/2 pounds top round steak, cut into strips
- Salt and pepper, to taste
- 1 medium onion, chopped
- 1 (10.5-ounce) can condensed cream of mushroom soup
- 1 pound fresh button mushrooms or 1 (8-ounce) can canned mushrooms, drained
- 1/4 cup water
- 1/4 cup white wine
- 1 tablespoon dried chives
- 1 clove garlic, minced
- 1 teaspoon Worcestershire sauce
- 1 cube beef bouillon
- 1 (16-ounce) container sour cream
- 1 tablespoon all-purpose flour
- 1/2 cup chopped fresh parsley
- 1 (8-ounce) package egg noodles

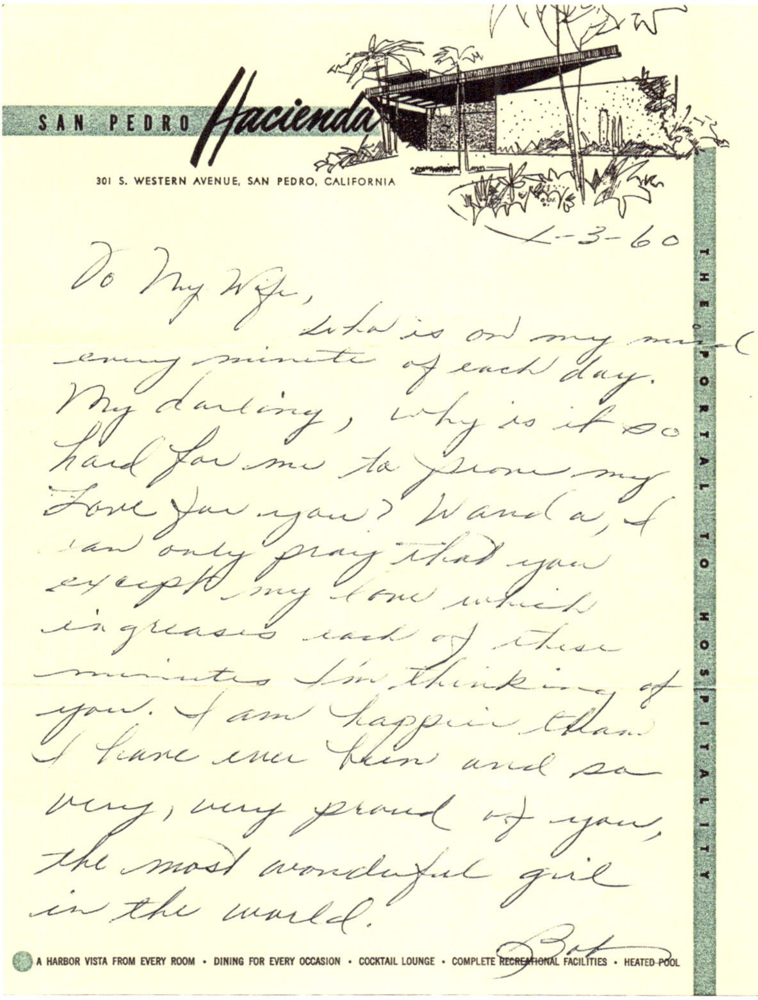

SAN PEDRO Hacienda

301 S. WESTERN AVENUE, SAN PEDRO, CALIFORNIA

THE PORTAL TO HOSPITALITY

1-3-60

To My Wife,

Who is on my mind every minute of each day. My darling, why is it so hard for me to prove my Love for you? Wanda, I can only pray that you except my love which ingreases each of these minutes I'm thinking of you. I am happier than I have ever been and so very, very proud of you, the most wonderful girl in the world.

Bob

A HARBOR VISTA FROM EVERY ROOM • DINING FOR EVERY OCCASION • COCKTAIL LOUNGE • COMPLETE RECREATIONAL FACILITIES • HEATED POOL

An early love letter dated January 3, 1960 from Bob to Wanda on the hotel stationary where they met.

SUMMER PASTA SALAD

RECIPE FROM JODY VINSON

METHOD

1. Cook ground chicken sausage in a large skillet with olive oil until it is just about cooked through and becomes browned and crumbly, about 7 to 10 minutes. Take off heat. Add salt and black pepper to taste. Set aside. Let cool completely.
2. Bring a large saucepan of water to a boil. Add the spiral pasta and cook for 10 minutes or until "al dente." Stir regularly to ensure the pasta does not stick. Drain, set aside, and let cool completely.
3. In a large bowl, combine cooled pasta and ground chicken sausage with the salami, cheese cubes, onion, and red pepper.
4. Toss and coat with salt, black pepper, and garlic powder
5. Season each serving to taste with balsamic vinegar and olive oil mixed together separately in a small bowl. Start with 1 part vinegar to 3 parts oil. If the balsamic is too acidic, add a small amount of honey to offset.
6. Serve cold.

YIELD: 10 TO 12 SERVINGS

INGREDIENTS

- 1/2 to 1 pound cooked and cooled ground chicken sausage
- 2 tablespoons olive oil
- Salt and black pepper, to taste
- 1 (16-ounce) boxes spiral pasta
- 1/4 pound thick cut Genoa salami, cut into cubes
- 1/4 pound pepper jack cheese, cut into cubes
- 1 medium white or red onion, diced
- 1 red pepper, diced
- Garlic powder, to taste
- Balsamic vinegar, to taste
- Olive oil, to taste, for dressing
- Honey, optional

TATER TOT CASSEROLE

RECIPE FROM JEANETTE HARSH

METHOD

1. Preheat oven to 350 degrees. Spray a 13x9-inch baking dish with nonstick cooking spray.
2. Cook ground beef and onion in a large skillet with olive oil until it is just about cooked through and becomes browned and crumbly, about 7 to 10 minutes. Drain fat and add the beef and onions to the baking dish.
3. In a separate large bowl, mix the mushroom soup, sour cream, dry mustard, corn, salt, and pepper together, then pour over the ground beef and onions. Stir until well mixed.
4. Cover with frozen tater tots and sprinkle the cheddar cheese over the top.
5. Bake for 1 hour.
6. Serve warm.

YIELD: ABOUT 8 SERVINGS

INGREDIENTS

- 1 and 1/2 pound ground beef
- 1 medium white onion, finely diced
- 2 tablespoons vegetable oil
- 1 (10.5-ounce) can condensed cream of mushroom soup
- 1 (16-ounce) container sour cream
- 1/4 teaspoon dry mustard
- 1 cup frozen corn
- Salt and black pepper, to taste
- 1 (32-ounce) package frozen tater tots
- 3/4 cup shredded cheddar cheese, for topping

TURKEY CHILI

RECIPE FROM CINDY SELL

METHOD

1. Heat olive oil in a stockpot over medium-high heat. Add the onion and cook for 2 minutes until the onion starts to soften. Add the ground turkey and cook, stirring to crumble the meat and until the turkey is browned, about 5 minutes. Add the garlic and cook, stirring, for 30 seconds.
2. Add the brown sugar, chili powder, cumin, oregano, salt, black pepper, and tomato paste. Stir to combine. Add the broth and stir, scraping up any bits from the bottom of the pot.
3. Stir in the tomatoes.
4. Bring to a boil, then reduce heat to low and simmer for 1 to 2 hours, stirring occasionally. Cover the chili for the first part of the cook time and uncover it for the last 30 minutes to thicken.
5. Add in beans for the last 15 minutes.
6. Taste and adjust salt if necessary.
7. Serve hot with toppings, as desired.
8. Store, covered in the fridge for up to 4 days, or in the freezer for up to 3 months.

YIELD: ABOUT 8 SERVINGS

Recommendation: Top with shredded cheese, sour cream or plain Greek yogurt, cilantro, chopped onions, etc.

Variation: This recipe tastes great with ground chicken instead of turkey.

INGREDIENTS

- 2 to 3 tablespoons olive oil
- 1 cup chopped yellow onion
- 1 pound ground turkey
- 4 cloves garlic, minced
- 1 tablespoon brown sugar
- 2 tablespoons chili powder
- 1 tablespoon ground cumin
- 1 teaspoon dried oregano
- 1/2 teaspoon salt
- 1/4 teaspoon black pepper
- 2 tablespoons tomato paste
- 1 and 3/4 cups chicken broth
- 1 (14-ounce) can fire roasted crushed tomatoes
- 1 (15-ounce) can kidney beans, rinsed and drained
- 1 (15-ounce) can black beans, rinsed and drained
- 1 (15-ounce) can pinto beans, rinsed and drained

TURKEY SOUP

METHOD

1. In a large saucepan over medium heat, saute the turkey with 2 tablespoons of olive oil until it is no longer pink; remove from the pan and set aside.
2. In the same pan, saute celery, carrots, and onions in the remaining olive oil.
3. Combine sautéed vegetables, cooked turkey, potatoes, tomatoes, beans, and broth into a stockpot. Cook on medium for 15 to 20 minutes.
4. Add salt and pepper to taste.
5. Store, covered in the fridge for up to 4 days, or in the freezer for up to 3 months.

YIELD: ABOUT 6 TO 8 SERVINGS

INGREDIENTS

- 1 pound ground turkey
- 4 tablespoons olive oil, divided
- 1 medium yellow onion, chopped
- 2 large celery sticks, chopped
- As many carrots as you want
- 3 large potatoes, diced
- 2 (14.5-ounce) cans chopped tomatoes, drained
- 1 (15.5-ounce) can cannellini beans, drained
- 1 (32-ounce) container chicken broth
- 2 cups water or more broth, if needed
- Salt and black pepper, to taste

WHITE CHICKEN CHILI

RECIPE FROM KAELIN SELL

INGREDIENTS

- 1 medium yellow onion, diced
- 1 to 2 medium bell peppers, diced
- 1 small jalapeño, seeds and membranes removed, finely diced
- 6 garlic cloves, minced
- 2 and 1/2 teaspoons ground cumin
- 1 teaspoon dried oregano
- 1 tablespoon chili powder
- 1 teaspoon salt, plus more to taste
- 1/2 teaspoon black pepper
- 1 and 1/2 pounds boneless, skinless chicken breasts or thighs
- 1 and 1/2 to 2 cups chicken broth
- 1 (14-ounce) can full-fat coconut milk
- 1 to 2 (14-ounce) cans of white beans, drained and rinsed
- Juice of 1/2 lime
- 1/2 cup chopped fresh cilantro

METHOD

1. Add the onion, peppers, garlic, and spices (cumin, oregano, chili powder, salt, and black pepper) to the bottom of a slow cooker. Arrange the chicken on top in a single layer.
2. Add the broth and place the lid on the slow cooker.
3. Set heat to low and cook for 5 to 6 hours or until the chicken is done and the vegetables are tender. About halfway through, stir the sauce and flip the chicken pieces over.
4. Remove the chicken from the slow cooker and shred it with two forks.
5. Return the shredded chicken to the slow cooker.
6. Turn the heat to high. Add the coconut milk and stir. Add the white beans. Replace the lid and continue heating for an additional 15 minutes.
7. Stir in the lime juice.
8. Taste and adjust seasonings as desired.
9. Serve hot, garnished with chopped cilantro and lime wedges, if desired.
10. Store, covered in the fridge for up to 4 days, or in the freezer for up to 3 months.

YIELD: 4 TO 6 SERVINGS

WHITEFISH CHEESE BAKE

RECIPE FROM MIDGE BROWN

METHOD

1. Preheat oven to 400 degrees.
2. Grease a 2-quart baking dish. Set aside.
3. Rinse fish and pat dry with a paper towel.
4. Put the onion, bell pepper, and garlic in a large skillet with 1 tablespoon of the oil and cook just until tender. Place the cooked vegetables into the prepared baking dish. Place the fish on top of the vegetables.
5. Bake uncovered for 10 minutes. Thicker fish will need closer to 20 minutes.
6. Combine the Parmesan cheese and breadcrumbs in a small bowl. Top the fish with sour cream, fresh lemon juice, and lemon-pepper seasoning. Sprinkle the cheese and breadcrumb mixture over the top.
7. Bake uncovered for 5 to 10 minutes or until the cheese and breadcrumbs start to brown. You can broil for the last couple of minutes.
8. Serve warm.

YIELD: 4 SERVINGS

INGREDIENTS

- 1 pound halibut, sole, cod, tilapia, or orange roughy, fresh or frozen, thawed
- 1 cup onion, chopped
- 1 cup red or green bell pepper, chopped
- 2 teaspoons bottled minced garlic
- 1 tablespoon vegetable oil plus more for frying
- 1/4 cup fine breadcrumbs
- Parmesan, Mexican blend, or cheddar cheese, freshly grated
- 1 (16-ounce) container of sour cream
- 1 teaspoon fresh lemon juice
- 1/2 teaspoon lemon-pepper seasoning

Every chapter of this book contains recipes from Wanda's family, and this chapter is no exception. From her niece Janet Kay's Bread and Butter Pickles to Bob Jr.'s family-famous coleslaw. Cindy would always make the Deviled Eggs for holiday gatherings. The Potato Salad is from Wanda's mom, Leona Inmon, affectionately known as Memaw.

It also includes some of Wanda's most celebrated dishes that her kids taste and go, "Yep, that's Mom's," such as the Potato Soup and the Sweet (Sweet) Potato Casserole.

One of my personal favorite holiday dishes is Green Bean Casserole with fried onions on top. As a family, we always use the recipe on the back of the Campbell's cream of mushroom soup can. For this book, I also wanted to include some new traditions with the old. The Green Bean Casserole recipe here is based on a version of the dish I had at my partner Noah's Thanksgiving gathering a few years ago. The fresh green beans in this version taste like eating a dish straight from the garden.

While writing this book, I kept asking myself, "What is the intention here?" What is the focus of this book? I realized, somewhere between recipe testing the dozenth cookie and purchasing my twentieth bag of sugar, that this book's main goal is to exist for the future generations of my family. For them to have a guide to all of our family food traditions, both new and old. To have a key to their family's past. This hope for the future made it important to include every recipe you see in this final copy, including those from both our given family and our chosen family, honoring old and creating new time-honored traditions.

This is how we lived, this is who we loved, and this is what we ate, together.

BLESS HER
PEA-PICKIN'
HEART

BREAD AND BUTTER PICKLES

RECIPE FROM JANET KAY

METHOD

1. Combine cucumbers and salt in a large bowl. Cover and chill for one to two hours in the fridge.
2. Strain cucumbers thoroughly under cold water. Drain well, and return the cucumbers to the bowl. Add onion to the bowl and toss with the cucumbers.
3. Combine both sugars, white vinegar, apple cider vinegar, mustard seeds, celery seeds, and ground turmeric in a medium saucepan. Bring to a simmer over medium heat, stirring until the sugar dissolves.
4. Once the sugar has dissolved, pour the hot vinegar mixture over the cucumber mixture. Let stand at room temperature for 1 hour.
5. Cover and refrigerate for 24 hours.
6. Store in an airtight container in the fridge for up to 1 month.

YIELD: 4 TO 6 CUPS

INGREDIENTS

- 2 pounds pickling cucumbers, sliced 1/4 inch thick
- 1 and 1/2 tablespoons salt
- 1 cup sweet onion, thinly sliced
- 1 cup granulated sugar
- 1/4 cup light brown sugar, firmly packed
- 1 cup white vinegar
- 1/2 cup apple cider vinegar
- 1 and 1/2 teaspoons yellow mustard seeds
- 1/2 teaspoon celery seeds
- 1/8 teaspoon ground turmeric

ROBERT SELL
Division Manager

Robert D. Sell joined the Directories Corporation as a Sales Representative with the Los Angeles Division in April, 1962. In 1967, he was promoted to District Sales Manager in Dallas, Texas, and won the Mel Hauser Award in 1972. In June, 1973, he was appointed Division Manager in Tampa, Florida, where he remained until January, 1980, transferring as Division Manager to the Camarillo Division. Effective in August, 1982, Bob was appointed Division Manager in the Seattle Division, and in January of 1984 he assumed the responsibilities of the combined Everett/Seattle Divisions. More recently the combined divisions were again separated. Bob was Division Manager of the Washington Seahawks Division until January, 1989, when he became the Division Manager for the Honolulu Division.

Wife: Wanda

An article celebrating some of Bob's achievements at GTE over the decades. He also worked for GTE in New York and Pennsylvania.

COLESLAW

RECIPE FROM BOB SELL JR.

METHOD

1. In a large bowl, whisk together mayonnaise, milk, buttermilk, sugar, salt, black pepper, lemon juice, and onion.
2. Add cabbage, carrots, and cilantro to the mixture. Toss to coat. Adjust ratios to taste, if needed.
3. Put in the fridge to set. Tastes best after 12 to 24 hours in the fridge.
4. Serve cold.
5. Store in an airtight container in the fridge for up to 5 days.

YIELD: 8 TO 10 SERVINGS

INGREDIENTS

- 3/4 cup mayonnaise
- 1/4 cup milk
- 1/4 cup buttermilk
- 3 tablespoons granulated sugar, more as needed
- Salt and black pepper, to taste
- 1 tablespoon fresh lemon juice
- 1 tablespoon finely shredded sweet onion
- 1/2 to 1 head of cabbage, washed and shredded
- 1 carrot, washed, peeled, and shredded
- 1/2 cup cilantro, coarsely chopped

COWGIRL CAVIAR

RECIPE FROM ANGELA VAUGHN

METHOD

1. Mix beans, peas, tomatoes, corn, onion, bell pepper, and jalapeno peppers in a large bowl.
2. Season with garlic salt. Add dressing and cilantro; toss to coat.
3. Refrigerate for 2 to 24 hours, or until ready to serve, allowing the vinegar to set into the ingredients for a better taste.
4. Serve cold with chips.
5. Store in an airtight container in the fridge for up to 5 days.

YIELD: 8 TO 10 SERVINGS

Recommendation: Resist the urge to add extra dressing to prevent the dip from getting soggy.

Variation: Add 3 Serrano peppers, peeled, seeded, and diced, for extra spice.

INGREDIENTS

- 1 (15.5-ounce) can of black beans,
- drained
- 1 (15.5-ounce) can black-eyed peas, drained
- 1 (14.5-ounce) can diced tomatoes, drained
- 1/2 medium red onion, chopped
- 2 cups frozen corn kernels, thawed
- 1/4 green bell pepper, finely chopped
- 1/2 cup chopped pickled jalapeño peppers
- 1/2 teaspoons garlic salt
- 1 cup Italian salad dressing
- 3/4 cup chopped cilantro

DEVILED EGGS WITH CAPERS

RECIPE FROM CINDY SELL

METHOD

1. Peel hard-cooked eggs and slice them in half lengthwise; scoop yolks into a small bowl.
2. Mash yolks with a fork.
3. Mix mashed yolk with remaining ingredients, and spoon into hollowed eggs.
4. Garnish with additional capers or fresh dill if desired. It will make more than enough filling for 12 egg halves, so save the extra yummy filling for topping toast, bagels, or whatever you'd like.
5. Store in an airtight container in the fridge for up to 2 days.

YIELD: 1 DOZEN

Recommendation: Resist the urge to add extra lemon juice to prevent the filling from becoming runny.

EGG BOILING AND CRACKING:

- Boil: Place 6 eggs in boiling water and boil for 10 minutes.
- Cool: After boiling, immediately transfer the eggs to an ice bath or under cold running water to stop the cooking process, making them easier to peel.
- Tap: Gently tap the egg all over on a hard surface.
- Roll: Roll the egg gently between your hands to loosen the shell.
- Peel: Begin peeling from the wider end of the egg, where the air pocket is located.
- Rinse: Peeling under running water or in an ice bath can help remove any stubborn shell pieces.

INGREDIENTS

- 6 eggs, hard cooked
- 1/3 cup mayonnaise
- 1 tablespoon finely chopped capers, plus more for garnish
- 1/4 teaspoon black pepper
- 1/4 teaspoon salt
- 2 teaspoons chopped fresh dill, plus more for garnish, optional
- 1 teaspoon Dijon mustard
- 1 teaspoon fresh lemon juice

GREEN BEAN CASSEROLE

RECIPE FROM DEAN AND LISA RAEL

METHOD

1. Preheat oven to 350 degrees. Spray a 13x9-inch baking dish with non-stick spray. Set aside.
2. Mix cream of mushroom soup, milk, and black pepper in a very large bowl.
3. Combine mixture with the green beans and 1 container of fried onions. Toss until evenly coated.
4. Place the mixture in the prepared baking dish and add another half container of onions to the top.
5. Bake for 60 to 75 minutes until heated through. After 15 minutes or so, cover the top with aluminum foil to prevent the onions from burning.
6. When the casserole is done, add as many remaining onions as desired to the top and cook for 5 more minutes or until crispy.
7. Serve hot.

INGREDIENTS

- 2 (10.5-ounce) cans condensed cream of mushroom soup
- 1 and 1/2 cups milk
- 1/4 teaspoon black pepper
- 2 (24-ounce) packages fresh green beans
- 2 (6-ounce) containers fried onion pieces

YIELD: 8 TO 10 SERVINGS

HOMINY CASSEROLE

RECIPE FROM CONNIE BEAM

METHOD

1. Preheat oven to 350 degrees.
2. Melt butter and milk in a microwave-safe bowl. Combine with all other ingredients in a casserole dish.
3. Bake for about 30 minutes. The casserole is done when the cheese is melted, bubbling, hot, and golden brown.
4. Sprinkle more cheese (as much as desired) on top, then return to the oven to brown the cheese.
5. Let cool slightly and serve.
6. Store leftovers covered in the fridge.

YIELD: ABOUT 12 SERVINGS

Variation: Add in chopped onions and garlic before baking.

INGREDIENTS

- 2 tablespoons butter
- 1/2 cup milk
- 1 can (25-ounce) hominy, drained and rinsed
- 1 (4-ounce) can chopped green chiles, drained
- 1/2 cup sour cream
- Salt and black pepper, to taste
- 1/2 cup shredded Monterey Jack cheese, plus more for topping

POTATO SALAD

RECIPE FROM LEONA INMON (MEMAW)

METHOD

1. Peel potatoes and cut into 3/4-inch to 1-inch cubed pieces.
2. Bring a large pot of water to boil. Add potatoes and a dash of salt, and partially cover with a lid. Boil until done, approximately 12 minutes. Drain and let cool.
3. While potatoes are cooling, chop onions, boiled eggs, celery, green peppers, and pickles.
4. When the potatoes have cooled, mix them with the chopped ingredients in a large bowl, then add Miracle Whip and mustard. Add salt and black pepper to taste.
5. If you make the salad ahead of time (the night before), you may need to add more Miracle Whip the next day, as potatoes can soak up the dressing.
6. Serve cold. Eat and enjoy.
7. Store in an airtight container in the fridge for 3 to 4 days.

INGREDIENTS

- 2 pounds Yukon Gold potatoes
- 1/4 cup chopped red, white, or yellow onion
- 3 large eggs, hard-boiled and chopped
- 2 medium stalks celery, chopped
- 1/4 cup chopped green peppers
- 1/4 cup chopped pickles (dill, kosher, or sour)
- 1/2 cup Miracle Whip
- 1/8 cup yellow mustard
- Salt and black pepper, to taste

YIELD: 6 TO 8 SERVINGS

POTATO SOUP

METHOD

1. In a large pot, boil and drain the potatoes.
2. In a skillet, fry the onions in the butter until the onions are soft but not browned.
3. Add drained potatoes to the large pot with fried onions and stir, then add milk. Bring the mixture to a slight bubble.
4. Remove the mixture from the stove top and throw it in a blender for a smoother texture. Then add it back into the large pot.
5. Add more milk to your preference to make it more soupy.
6. Add salt and black pepper to taste.
7. Serve hot.
8. Store leftovers in the fridge. Potatoes will soak up most of the liquid overnight, so you may need to add more milk when reheating.

INGREDIENTS

- 2 medium russet potatoes, peeled and cubed
- 1/4 cup white or sweet onions, chopped
- 1 tablespoon butter
- 1 and 3/4 cup milk, more to taste as needed
- Salt and black pepper, to taste

YIELD: ABOUT 2 SERVINGS

Recommendation: Use this as a base for a loaded potato soup. Add toppings such as bacon, chives, cheese, etc.

SCALLOPED POTATOES

RECIPE FROM TERRISA SELL

METHOD

1. Preheat oven to 375 degrees. Grease a 13x9-inch baking dish and set aside.
2. In a large saucepan, cook onions with butter.
3. Stir in flour, salt, and pepper; add milk and cook until thick and bubbly.
4. Add cheese and cook until melted.
5. Pour half of the potatoes into the prepared baking dish, followed by half of the sauce, and repeat. Cover the dish with a lid or aluminum foil.
6. Bake for 45 minutes, covered.
7. Uncover the dish and stir once. Turn the oven down to 350 degrees and bake for another 30 minutes, uncovered.
8. Let cool slightly and serve warm.
9. Store, covered, in the fridge for up to 3 days.

YIELD: 8 TO 10 SERVINGS

INGREDIENTS

- 1/4 cup yellow or white onion, chopped
- 1/4 cup (1/2 stick) butter or margarine
- 1/4 cup all-purpose flour
- 2 and 1/2 cups milk
- Salt and black pepper, to taste
- 3/4 cup shredded cheddar cheese
- 5 large Yukon Gold or peeled russet potatoes, thinly sliced

SOUTHERN HUSH PUPPIES

RECIPE FROM ANGELA VAUGHN

METHOD

1. In a large mixing bowl, combine the cornmeal, flour, sugar, baking powder, salt, and cayenne pepper.
2. In a separate large bowl, whisk together the egg and buttermilk. Add the dry ingredients to the egg mixture, stirring until combined.
3. Heat 2 inches of oil over medium-high heat in a large cast-iron skillet. When hot, carefully drop rounded spoonfuls of batter into the hot oil. Fry for 2 to 3 minutes, turning partway through, until the hush puppies are golden brown on each side.
4. Remove the hush puppies from the oil and transfer to a paper towel to drain.
5. Eat warm.

INGREDIENTS

- 1 cup cornmeal
- 1/2 cup all-purpose flour, leveled
- 2 tablespoons granulated sugar
- 1 and 1/2 teaspoons baking powder
- 1/2 teaspoon salt
- 1/4 teaspoon cayenne pepper
- 1 egg, lightly beaten
- 3/4 cup buttermilk
- Vegetable oil, for frying

YIELD: 1 TO 2 DOZEN HUSH PUPPIES, DEPENDING ON THEIR SIZE.

SWEET (SWEET) POTATO CASSEROLE

METHOD

1. Preheat the oven to 350 degrees. Butter a 1-quart casserole dish. Set aside. Line a baking sheet with foil and spray it with cooking spray.
2. Prick the sweet potatoes all over with a fork, then place them on the prepared baking sheet. Bake for 45 minutes to 1 hour, until soft.
3. Let the potatoes cool, scooping out the insides into a large bowl, leaving the skins behind. Mix in the eggs, sugar, butter, vanilla extract, and milk. Pour the mixture into the prepared casserole dish.
4. In a large bowl, mix brown sugar, butter, and flour for the topping until it resembles cornmeal. Spread it over the top of the potato mixture.
5. Cover with chopped pecan halves and pat down with your hand.
6. Bake for 45 minutes, until heated all the way through and the topping begins to brown.
7. Remove the sweet potato casserole from the oven and sprinkle with mini marshmallows. Set the oven to broil, then return the casserole to the oven and cook just long enough for the marshmallows to toast on top.
8. Serve warm.
9. Store, covered, in the fridge.

YIELD: ABOUT 10 SERVINGS

INGREDIENTS

- 3 pounds sweet potatoes (about 12 small or 6 large), peeled and cut into large pieces
- 2 eggs
- 1 cup granulated sugar
- 6 tablespoons butter, softened
- 1 tablespoon vanilla extract
- 1/2 cup milk

TOPPING

- 1 cup firmly packed brown sugar
- 2 tablespoons butter, softened
- 1/3 cup all-purpose flour
- 1 cup chopped pecans
- 2 cups mini marshmallows

In 2020, my Aunt Cindy gave Wanda a journal, prefilled with prompts and questions about her likes, dislikes, and important memories. After Wanda passed, Cindy came back into possession of the journal. Every once in a while, she will share entries with the family. Here is one of my favorites.

Mom, what is your perfect day?

Relaxing in the sunshine with a glass of iced tea and a book.

Spending a holiday with all my children and grandchildren, having fun.

TO WET
YOUR
WHISTLE

AMARETTO

METHOD

1. Bring water to a boil.
2. Add sugar and cook until a candy thermometer inserted in the liquid reaches 225 degrees. Without a candy thermometer, drop a small amount into ice-cold water. When ready, the syrup will form a loose, thin thread.
3. Let cool for 30 minutes.
4. Stir and add to brandy. Let cool completely.
5. Add almond and vanilla extracts. Stir to combine, and serve in small glasses or pour into coffee.
6. Store in an airtight glass container in a cool, dark place. Drink within 6 months.

INGREDIENTS

- 2 cups water
- 4 and 1/2 cups granulated sugar
- 1-liter brandy
- 2 tablespoons almond extract
- 2 tablespoons vanilla extract

YIELD: 3 TO 4 DOZEN SERVINGS

Recommendation: A candy thermometer is helpful for this recipe, but not necessary.

CHOCOLATE SAUCE

METHOD

1. In a medium saucepan, add evaporated milk and sugar. Add baking chocolate, baking cocoa, and corn syrup.
2. Bring to a rolling boil over medium heat, stirring with a whisk. Stir frequently as it comes to a boil. Stir constantly once it is at a rolling boil. Let boil for 2 minutes.
3. Turn off the heat. Add butter to the mixture. Whisk until melted.
4. Add vanilla extract and salt.
5. Let the hot fudge sauce sit at room temperature for 15 to 20 minutes to cool and thicken.
6. Store in an airtight container in the fridge for up to 3 days.

YIELD: 3 CUPS

INGREDIENTS

- 1 (12-ounce) can evaporated milk
- 1 and 3/4 cups granulated sugar
- 4 ounces unsweetened baking chocolate, broken up
- 2 tablespoons baking cocoa
- 1/4 cup light corn syrup
- 2 tablespoons salted butter
- 1 teaspoon vanilla extract
- 1/2 teaspoon salt

DILL DIP

METHOD

1. The night before or the morning of that you plan to serve, combine all ingredients in a medium bowl.
2. Cover and let sit in the refrigerator for 2 to 8 hours.
3. Before serving, top with more green onions.
4. Serve cold with fresh vegetables or crackers.
5. Store in an airtight container in the fridge for up to 5 days.

YIELD: ABOUT 2 CUPS

Variation: Mix chopped pickles into the dip. Make pickles following the Bread and Butter Pickles recipe (page 186).

INGREDIENTS

- 1 cup sour cream
- 1 cup mayonnaise
- 2 tablespoons fresh dill
- 1 teaspoon chopped parsley
- 1/3 teaspoon celery salt
- 1/3 teaspoon white sugar
- 1/3 teaspoon onion powder
- 3 green onions, chopped, plus more for topping
- Salt, to taste

HOT CHOCOLATE

METHOD

1. Whisk together the baking cocoa, sugar, and salt in a small bowl.
2. Heat a large saucepan over medium-high heat. Pour 1 cup of the milk into the warmed saucepan and add the baking cocoa and sugar mixture. Whisk until smooth and all lumps are removed.
3. Add the remaining milk and whisk together well. Heat the hot chocolate mixture until very warm, but do not boil.
4. Remove the hot chocolate from the heat and add the milk chocolate. Mix until the chocolate is melted. Add vanilla if desired.
5. Pour the hot chocolate into mugs and enjoy!
6. Store in an airtight container in the fridge for 3 to 5 days.

INGREDIENTS

- 1/4 cup baking cocoa
- 1/4 teaspoon salt
- 1/2 cup granulated sugar
- 4 cups milk, divided
- 1 and 1/2 tablespoons milk chocolate bar
- Dash of vanilla extract, optional

YIELD: 4 SERVINGS

SALSA

RECIPE FROM TIM ARWOOD

METHOD

1. Put tomatoes and peppers in a medium to large pot with about an inch of water over the top of them and bring to a boil. Boil until soft, 10 to 20 minutes. When you boil the tomatoes, the skin will start to come off; that's when they are about ready. The pepper won't get very soft, but you want to ensure they get softer than they start, or they won't blend easily.
2. After boiling, throw all ingredients into a blender. Put the tomatoes in when they are drippy; that will be enough water. Pulse and quickly let blend for a couple of seconds, then back to pulsing.
3. Serve cool. Add cilantro on top.
4. Store in an airtight container in the fridge for 5 to 7 days.

INGREDIENTS

- 4 to 6 Roma tomatoes
- 3 Serrano peppers, peeled and seeded
- 1 medium to large sweet or yellow onion, diced
- 1/4 to 1/2 teaspoon salt
- 3 cloves garlic, minced
- Cilantro, for garnish

YIELD: ABOUT 4 CUPS

SALSA VERDE

RECIPE FROM MATT SISSERSON

METHOD

1. Boil tomatillos in water, then pan fry or broil in the oven until soft enough to peel the outer membrane off. Skin will blacken, and that's okay. It will make taking the skin off easy, and it will add some flavor.
2. Boil peppers in oil or water until soft enough to peel the outer membrane off. You could also char the pepper to do this.
3. Once tomatillos and peppers are cool to touch, peel off outer membranes.
4. Blend all ingredients until smooth.
5. Serve once cooled.
6. Store in an airtight container in the fridge for up to 7 days.

YIELD: ABOUT 4 CUPS

INGREDIENTS

- 1 pound tomatillos
- 3 to 5 serrano peppers, seeded
- 1 bunch cilantro
- 4 to 6 garlic cloves, minced
- 1 small yellow onion, diced
- Juice of 1/2 a lemon or lime
- Salt and black pepper, to taste

SPICED TEA

RECIPE FROM WANDA HENDERSON, GTE

METHOD

1. Pour water into a large pot and add all ingredients except tea bags.
2. Bring to a boil.
3. Reduce heat, add tea packages to the water. Cover and simmer for several hours.
4. Remove and discard cloves, cinnamon stick, and tea bags.
5. Serve hot.
6. To store, let cool to room temperature. Put in an airtight container in the fridge for 3 to 5 days.

YIELD: ABOUT 3 TO 4 DOZEN SERVINGS

INGREDIENTS

- 1/2 gallon cran-apple juice
- 1/2 gallon hot water
- 6 to 8 whole cloves
- 4 ounces frozen orange juice concentrate
- 3 to 5 cinnamon sticks
- 4 black tea bags

STEAK MARINADE

RECIPE FROM CINDY SELL

METHOD

1. Combine ingredients in a large plastic zipper top bag.
2. Shake it up well. Add up to 1 pound of meat to the bag and marinate for at least 6 hours.
3. Cook meat by preferred method.
4. Discard marinade after meat has marinated.

YIELD: UP TO 1 POUND OF UNCOOKED STEAK

INGREDIENTS

- 1/4 cup olive oil
- 1/4 cup balsamic vinegar
- 3 to 4 garlic cloves, minced
- 1 teaspoon salt
- Crushed chipotle pepper flakes, to your taste

STRAWBERRY JAM

Recipe from Jordana Spaseff née Popova

METHOD

1. Rinse and mash berries. The more you puree the berries, the fewer fruit chunks will be in the final jam.
2. Put mashed berries in a stockpot and bring to a boil. Boil for 3 minutes, stirring occasionally. Remove berries from the burner, and stir in half of the sugar.
3. Return to the burner and boil for 3 more minutes, stirring occasionally.
4. Remove from the burner again and stir in the remaining sugar, stirring occasionally.
5. Boil for 3 more minutes.
6. Remove from the burner. If there are still too many fruit chunks for your liking, mix with an electric mixer. Let cool.
7. Once cool, jar and refrigerate or freeze.

YIELD: 2 TO 3 PINTS OF JAM

INGREDIENTS

- 4 pounds (8 cups) strawberries, hulled and roughly chopped
- 6 cups granulated sugar, divided

33

SWEET TEA

METHOD

1. In a large saucepan, bring water to a boil and then remove from heat. Add tea bags and steep for 10 to 25 minutes, depending on the strength you want.
2. Remove tea bags.
3. Add sugar while the tea is hot. Add at least 1/3 cup and maybe more, depending on what your sweet spot is. Stir to allow sugar to dissolve.
4. Refrigerate.
5. Serve over ice with lemon wedges.

Drink all day. Make more.
Add more sugar.

YIELD: ABOUT 8 SERVINGS

INGREDIENTS

- 1 and 1/2 quart water
- 3 black tea bags
- 1/3 cup granulated sugar (at least)
- 1 lemon

While going through my grandma's recipe box and asking family members about their favorite recipes, I laughed and dry-heaved at some of the discoveries – a formidable combination to do at the same time.

Here are a few recipes that should be left in the past, but I am including them because they were (in some cases, still are) family favorites. If one of these toots your horn, no judgment from me. I still eat like a 12-year-old on most days. #girldinner

Both my grandpa and my uncle loved Cream Tuna. Uncle Bob still makes this dish. Jacobe and Kaelin hilariously call this "hobo food." Growing up in Bob Jr.'s house, the smell of fish and bacon grease filled their home. As Pops would say, "It'll put hair on your chest."

Nana and Pops loved Liver and Onions. Perhaps after an evening of enjoying a show at the drive-in movie theater, sans seatbelts, and dancing the jitterbug with pennies in our loafers, this would be a delicious dish.

Raisin Pie, folks. Many people, including one of my aunts, still love it. The recipe card I found has someone's handwriting stating, "Leave out the raisins." I suspect this was my mom. Like mother, like daughter.

The recipe for Rice Patties is a historical one. I learned from Aunt Angie that during the Depression, when you're poor in the South and raising a large family, this was an easy and inexpensive way to make a delicious dessert.

Milk Toast was one of my grandpa's favorite desserts. It's not so bad, although I don't have positive connotations with wet bread. I mean, do you?

Lucky for you, I left out the Shrimp Dip Jello Mold made with a can of tomato soup. Bummer? Something to look forward to in the next book.

FOR
PETE'S
SAKE

CREAM TUNA

METHOD

1. In a medium skillet, mix bacon grease and tuna on high heat. Add flour while hot to make a roux.
2. On high heat, add milk, stirring constantly. Simmer, adding additional milk as needed, until the desired thickness is reached. Add salt to taste.
3. Pour gravy over toast.
4. Sprinkle with black pepper and serve with a tall glass of milk.
5. Not recommended to store, eat hot.

YIELD: 2 SERVINGS

INGREDIENTS

- 2 to 4 tablespoons bacon grease or shortening
- 1 (5-ounce) can tuna in water, drained
- 3 tablespoons all-purpose flour
- 1 cup milk, or more as needed
- Salt and black pepper, to taste
- 2 to 4 pieces of toast

LIVER AND ONIONS

INGREDIENTS

- 4 pieces of beef liver, 2 and 1/2 to 3 pounds each
- 1 teaspoon garlic powder
- 1/2 teaspoon onion powder
- 2 tablespoons all-purpose flour
- Salt and black pepper, to taste
- 2 tablespoons vegetable oil
- 1 large onion, sliced into rings
- 2 cups beef broth

METHOD

1. Rinse the beef liver and pat it dry.
2. In a small bowl, combine the garlic powder, onion powder, flour, salt, and black pepper to taste. Use it to season both sides of the liver.
3. Heat the vegetable oil in a large skillet over medium-high heat.
4. Sear both sides of the liver until browned, then set aside and keep warm.
5. Add the sliced onions to the skillet and reduce the heat to medium. Cook until the onions have softened.
6. Stir the beef broth into the skillet with the onions.
7. Place the liver into the broth and onions.
8. Bring to a low boil and cook for 15 minutes before serving.
9. Eat warm.
10. Store in an airtight container in the fridge or freezer after the dish has completely cooled.

YIELD: 4 SERVINGS

MILK TOAST

METHOD

1. Toast the bread and break into pieces over a bowl.
2. Pour warm milk over the toast.
3. Sprinkle with sugar, to taste. Serve warm.
4. Not recommended to store.

INGREDIENTS

- 1 to 2 slices of white bread
- 3/4 cup warm milk
- Granulated sugar, to taste

YIELD: 1 SERVING

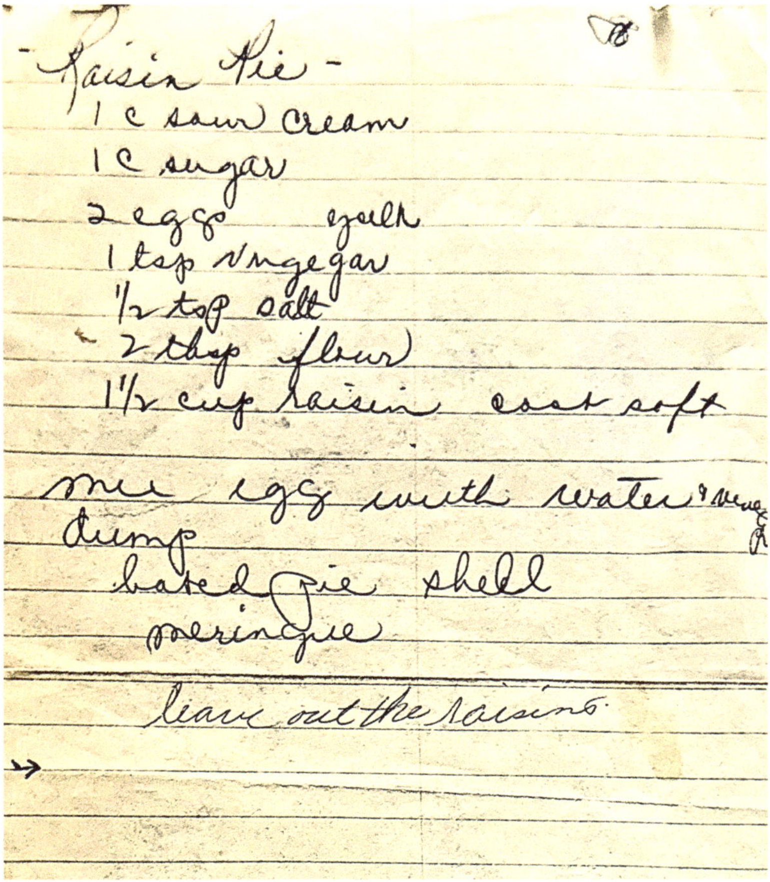

- Raisin Pie -

1 c sour cream
1 c sugar
2 eggs yolk
1 tsp vinegar
½ tsp salt
2 tbsp flour
1½ cup raisin cook soft

mix egg with water & vinegar
dump
baked pie shell
meringue

leave out the raisins

Original Raisin Pie recipe.

RAISIN PIE

METHOD

1. Prepare pie crust.
2. Lower the oven to 350 degrees.
3. In a 1-quart saucepan, heat raisins and water to a boil; reduce heat and simmer for 5 minutes. Drain; set aside.
4. In a 2-quart saucepan, mix sugar, flour, and salt.
5. In a medium bowl, beat egg yolks, sour cream, and margarine. Combine into the saucepan. Cook over low heat for about 15 minutes or until thick, similar to a pudding texture. Remove from heat. Add drained raisins, nuts, and vanilla extract. Pour into baked pie shell.
6. Meringue:
   - In a large bowl, beat egg whites and cream of tartar with an electric mixer until foamy.
   - Gradually add sugar, beating until mixture forms stiff peaks, which looks like whipped cream.
   - Mix in vanilla extract.
   - Spoon meringue over filling and spread to the edge of the crust.
7. Place the pie on the middle oven rack, with a sheet of foil or a cookie sheet on the rack below it in case of spillover. Bake for about 12 minutes, or until the meringue is lightly browned.
8. Cool completely, about 3 hours.
9. Store for up to 2 days covered on the counter or in the fridge for up to 4 days.

YIELD: 10 TO 12 SERVINGS

INGREDIENTS

- 1 parbaked pie crust
- 1 cup raisins
- 1 and 1/4 cups water
- 1 cup granulated sugar
- 3 tablespoons all-purpose flour
- 1/2 teaspoon salt
- 3 eggs, divided
- 1 cup sour cream
- 2 tablespoons margarine or butter, softened
- 1 cup chopped walnuts or pecans
- 1 teaspoon vanilla extract

MERINGUE

- 3 egg whites
- 1/4 teaspoon cream of tartar
- 1 teaspoon granulated sugar for each egg white
- 1 teaspoon vanilla extract

RAISIN PIE

PIE CRUST

INGREDIENTS

- 1 cup all-purpose flour
- 1/2 cup shortening
- 1/2 teaspoon salt
- 1/8 to 1/4 cup ice water

METHOD

1. Combine flour, shortening, and salt with a pastry cutter until shortening is in small, manageable chunks. Do not overwork the dough.
2. Slowly add in ice water with one hand while continuing to form the dough into a ball with the other hand. Use as much ice water as needed until the dough comes together nicely into a ball. Do not overwork the dough.
3. Flour your countertop or breadboard. Put the dough on the floured surface and shape into a ball.
4. Flatten the dough into a disk. Sprinkle flour on top of the dough. Roll out with a rolling pin to the desired size.
5. Line a pie pan with the dough and pinch out the crust. Since you are parbaking the crust, prick all over the bottom and sides of the pie crust with a fork and bake using pie weights.
6. Bake for 15 to 20 minutes at 425 degrees.

RICE PATTIES

METHOD

1. Combine rice, egg, baking powder, and flour. Shape into 2 patties.
2. In a large skillet, heat the vegetable oil until glistening. Fry the patties until golden brown, about 3 to 4 minutes per side.
3. Serve warm with prepared My-T-Fine Lemon Instant Pudding Mix and Pie Filling on top.
4. Not recommended to store.

YIELD: 2 SERVINGS

INGREDIENTS

- 1 to 1 and 1/2 cup of day-old cooked rice
- 1 egg
- 1 teaspoon baking powder
- 3 tablespoons all-purpose flour
- 2 tablespoons vegetable oil
- 1 (3.4-ounce) box My-T-Fine Lemon Instant Pudding Mix and Pie Filling, prepared to box instructions

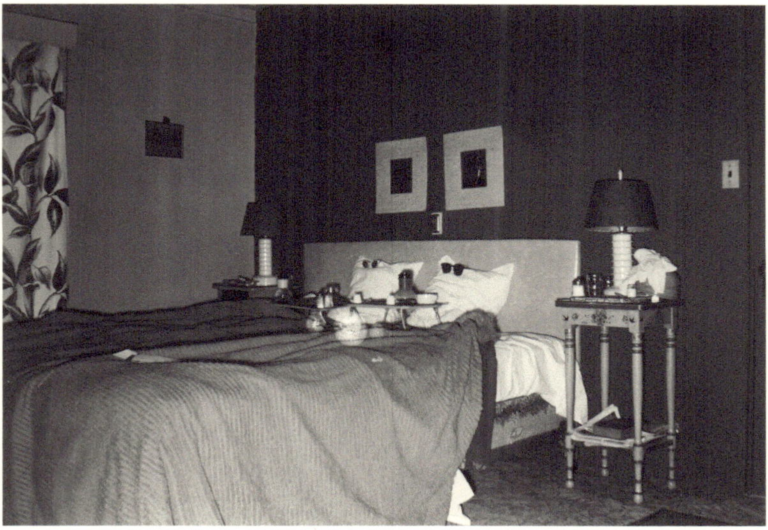

This is one of my favorite pictures from Bob and Wanda's honeymoon camera roll, and possibly all time.

Peanut Butter
1 cup white
1 cup brown
1 cup peanut
1 cup shortening
2 eggs beaten
2 1/2 cups sifted
Fudge Cookies
Potatoe Salad
Peel potatoes & cut in cubed pieces. Cook in water to cover til done (not mushy)
Chop onion
Chop Eggs (boiled)
Chop celery
Chop green peppers
Chop pickles
Peanut Blossoms
Sift together:
1 3/4 cup sifted
1 tsp soda
1/2 tsp salt
Cream:
1/2 cup shortening
1/2 cup peanut butter
1/2 cup sugar
From Texas... With Love
Brownies
1 cup flour
16 oz can Hershey choc syrup
1 tsp vanilla
1 cup chopped nuts
30-40 mins.
Tomatillos 1 lb
• Boil in water or oil until soft enough to peel outer thin membrane off
Bushell of cilantro
Garlic 4-6 minced cloves
Onion yellow 1/2 diced
Serrano peppers 3-5
• Boil in oil or water until soft enough to peel outer thin membrane off
• You could also char the pepper to do it
Dash of lemon or lime juice
Salt/pepper to taste, needs a fair amount of salt for taste but isn't absolutely necessary. Add to your own taste
Blend all

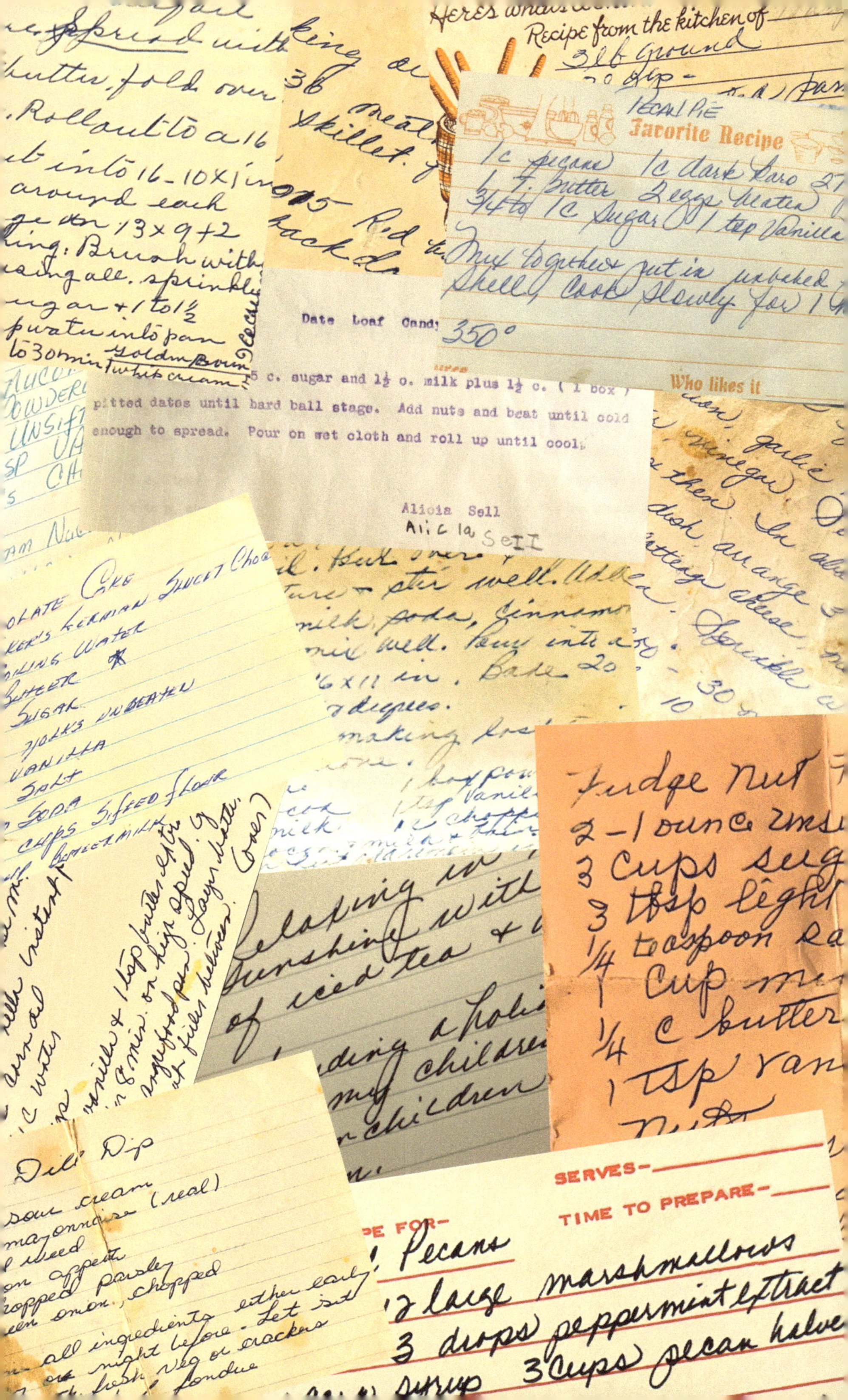

Recipe from the kitchen of
Pecan Pie
Favorite Recipe
1 c pecans 1 c dark karo
Mix together + put in unbaked
350°
Who likes it
Date Loaf Candy
5 c. sugar and 1½ c. milk plus 1½ c. (1 box)
pitted dates until hard ball stage. Add nuts and beat until cold
enough to spread. Pour on wet cloth and roll up until cool.
Alicia Sell
Fudge Nut
3 cups sugar
1 tsp van
Dill Dip
sour cream
mayonnaise (real)
SERVES-
TIME TO PREPARE-
Pecans
3 drops peppermint extract
3 cups pecan halves

Wanda on the Washington Coast under a rainbow.

LEFTOVERS

I LOOKED YOU UP IN THE DICTIONARY

Favorite Bob & Wanda family sayings.

Bless her pea-pickin' heart a genuine expression of sympathy, empathy, or concern for someone's well-being. The imagery of "pea-pickin'" refers to the act of picking peas, often associated with rural, simple, or humble activities. Thus, the phrase can imply that the speaker feels affectionate pity for the person being addressed, acknowledging their innocence or lack of awareness in a lighthearted manner. It's used in a playful or teasing context.

Cool cat An old-fashioned slang term that describes someone fashionable, stylish, or calm and composed.

Dagnabbit An old-fashioned, informal American exclamation expressing anger or surprise. For example, "Dagnabbit! Wanda! Have you seen my keys?"

Darn Tootin' Correct! Right! For example, "Is that banana bread any good?" "You're darn tootin'!"

Different A 'polite' if not slightly passive-aggressive way to say you don't like something, someone, or someplace. "That's different."

Don't be ugly To be kind, respectful, and avoid being mean or hateful, regardless of appearance. It's a reminder that inner character matters more than outward looks.

Easy as pie Very easy, "a piece of cake."

For Pete's sake Used to express frustration, exasperation, or annoyance, acting as a euphemism for "for God's sake" or "for Christ's sake."

Funny as all get out An expression that means extremely funny or ridiculously amusing.

Golly, gee An exclamation used to express surprise or wonder.

Grandma Granatelli or Lead Foot You put the pedal to the metal while driving. For example, "Lead Foot Wanda."

Hey, sexy! A term of endearment, a greeting when you haven't seen someone you love in a while. A phrase not everyone can say with the same air of inoffensiveness and bravado as Pops.

Hoopa Doopa To show excitement; synonyms: cool, awesome, yahoo, let's go!

I'll high-five ya A polite response when you don't feel like kissing or hugging someone when they ask you for a hug or a kiss.

I looked you up in the dictionary... A way to start a playful insult or compliment.

Keep your nose clean Stay out of trouble.

Nothing to write home about A way of saying something is ordinary, unexceptional, or not particularly good or exciting.

Ommie Wanda's niece Connie, only three years younger than she was, nicknamed her this as kids. Wanda called her Tooter in return.

Pretty is as pretty does A person's true beauty is revealed through their actions and character, not just their physical appearance. Grandma Harsh would say this.

Pull my finger A joke that involves a prankster asking you to pull their finger, which produces an unexpected noise and smell.

It will put hair on your chest A humorous way of saying something is strong, satisfying, or good for you, often referring to a drink, meal, or experience.

Slick as a whistle Something is done very smoothly and expertly, or that a person is skilled and efficient in doing something.

Tall drink of water A compliment, implying attractiveness or desirability of a tall man, for example, "He's a tall drink of water."

There's always tomorrow A saying used to offer hope and encouragement, suggesting that even if today didn't go as planned, there's another opportunity to try again in the future.

Twee-twat Your rear end, for example, "I'm going to get your twee-twat." often said in response to sneaking mouthfuls of dessert in the kitchen before dinner.

Two Peas in a Pod Two people that look, act, or seem extremely similar. It can also mean that the people are emotionally very close.

Wide-Turn What you call someone when they swing their car to the left before making a right turn. AKA what Pops called me after teaching me how to drive. "Lookout, here comes Wide-Turn."

What a hoot Something is very amusing or funny.

What it is To show how much you like something; synonyms: looking good, I approve, that's cool. It can also be used as a greeting when entering a room.

You're kidding me Wow! No way! Amazing.

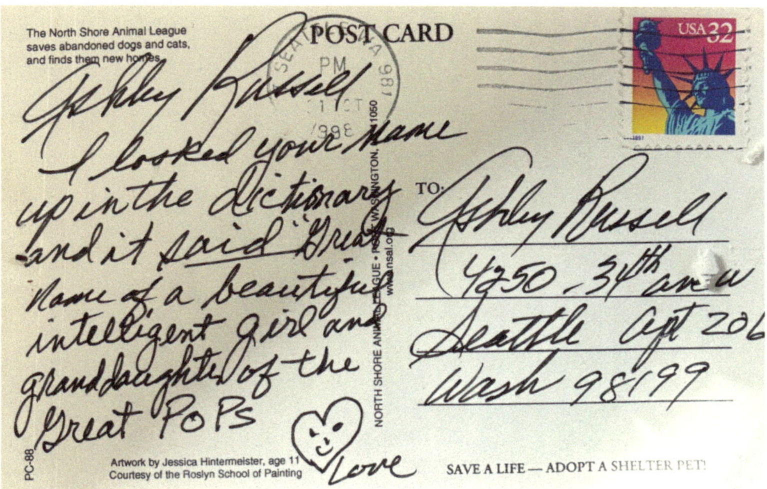

Postcard from Pops to Ashley, 1998.

WANDA MAE

GRANDPARENTS

WILLIAM J. INMON AND
CYNTHIA E. SHANNON
RODNEY B. BEARDEN AND
MARTHA ANN MOORE

PARENTS

LOYF DAVID INMON AND
LEONA (LONIE) BEARDEN

AUNT AND UNCLE

THELMA AND HUBERT

BROTHERS

KENNETH B, WELDON,
PRESTON, AND WC

SISTERS

WYNONA, DOROTHY, AND
MARILYN

NIECES AND NEPHEWS

CONNIE, JANET KAY, MIKE, GEORGE,
RANDALL, RICHARD, SHARON, KARON,
KENNETH RAY, SHELIA, SANDRA FAY,
PAT, RICHARD M., GARY, AND MIKE S.

GREAT NIECES AND NEPHEWS

LEIGHANNE,
MIKE, JAMES,
GREG, DAVID,
WESLEY,
JEREMY,
BRANDON,
VANESSA,
JAMES,
CHRISTOPHER,
JASON, SCOTT,
MICHELLE,
KIMBERLY,
MICHAEL RAY
JR., DEBBIE,
KIM, KENNY,
SHAWN, DAVID,
SEAN, KANDI,
JEFFREY, AND
JOHN

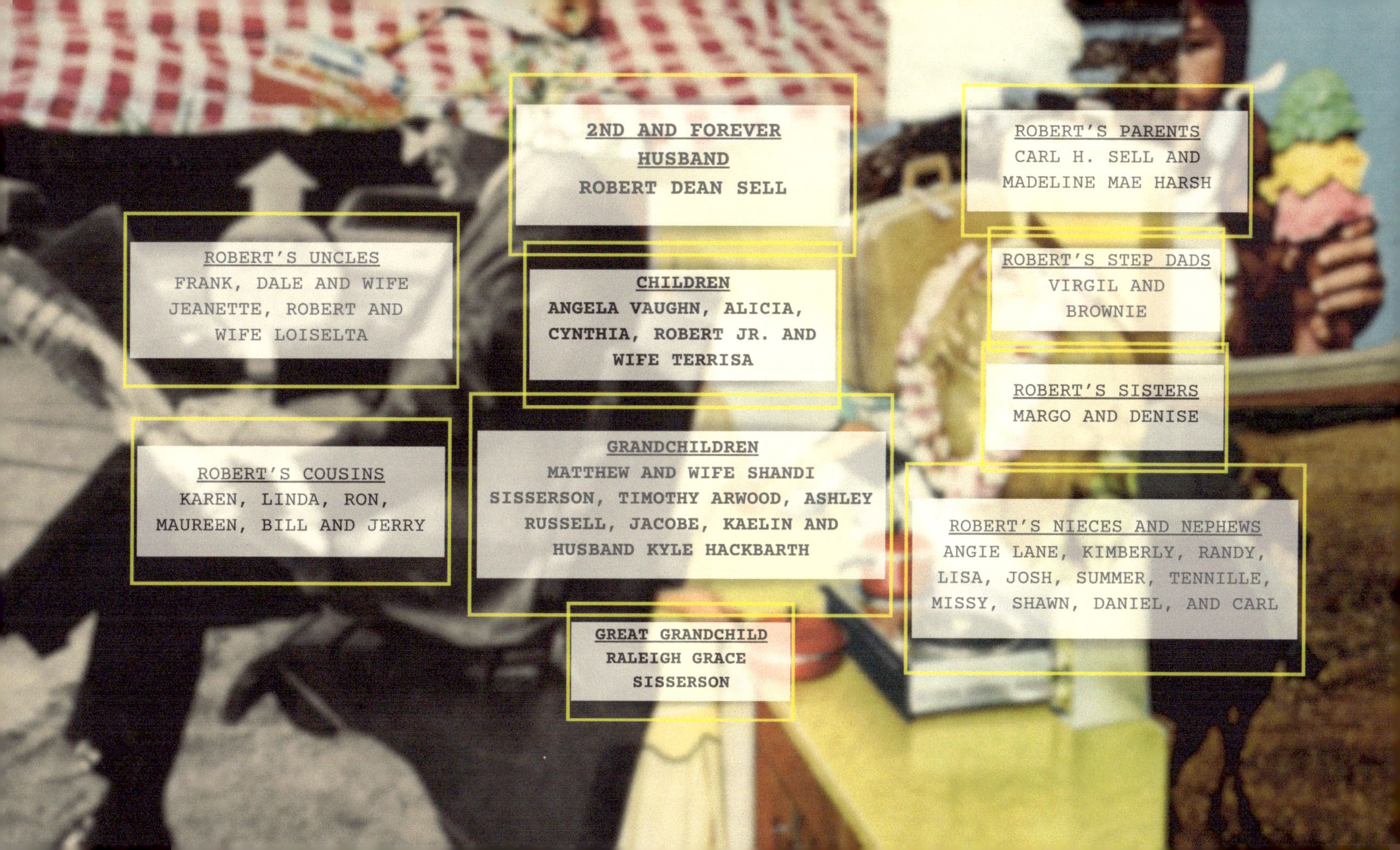
ROBERT'S UNCLES
FRANK, DALE AND WIFE JEANETTE, ROBERT AND WIFE LOISELTA
ROBERT'S COUSINS
KAREN, LINDA, RON, MAUREEN, BILL AND JERRY
2ND AND FOREVER HUSBAND
ROBERT DEAN SELL
CHILDREN
ANGELA VAUGHN, ALICIA, CYNTHIA, ROBERT JR. AND WIFE TERRISA
GRANDCHILDREN
MATTHEW AND WIFE SHANDI SISSERSON, TIMOTHY ARWOOD, ASHLEY RUSSELL, JACOBE, KAELIN AND HUSBAND KYLE HACKBARTH
GREAT GRANDCHILD
RALEIGH GRACE SISSERSON
ROBERT'S PARENTS
CARL H. SELL AND MADELINE MAE HARSH
ROBERT'S STEP DADS
VIRGIL AND BROWNIE
ROBERT'S SISTERS
MARGO AND DENISE
ROBERT'S NIECES AND NEPHEWS
ANGIE LANE, KIMBERLY, RANDY, LISA, JOSH, SUMMER, TENNILLE, MISSY, SHAWN, DANIEL, AND CARL

THYME TO DANCE

Listen to these Bob and Wanda favorites while you cut a rug in the kitchen!

Somewhere Over the Rainbow - Judy Garland 1939
You Are My Sunshine - Jimmie Davis 1940
Hey, Good Lookin' - Hank Williams 1951
That's Amore - Dean Martin 1953
Mr. Sandman - The Chordettes 1954
Lawdy Miss Clawdy - Lloyd Price 1952
Red Hot - Billy Lee Riley 1957
Walkin' After Midnight - Patsy Cline 1957
You Send Me - Sam Cooke 1957
Good Golly Miss Molly - Little Richard 1958
Yakety Yak - The Coasters 1958
Itsy Bitsy Teeny Weeny Yellow Polka Dot Bikini - Brian Hyland 1960
Route 66 - Chuck Berry 1961
Can't Help Falling in Love - Elvis Presley 1961
I Want to Hold Your Hand - The Beatles 1963
Pink Panther Theme Song - Composed by Henry Mancini 1964
I Got You (I Feel Good) - James Brown 1964
Oh, Pretty Woman - Roy Orbison 1964
L-O-V-E - Nat King Cole 1964
King of the Road - Roger Miller 1965
These Boots are Made for Walking - Nancy Sinatra 1966
Ain't No Mountain High Enough - Marvin Gaye and Tammi Terrell 1967
My Way - Frank Sinatra 1969
Spooky - Dusty Springfield 1970
Amazing Grace - Aretha Franklin 1972
Chantilly Lace - Jerry Lee Lewis 1972
Zip-A-Dee-Doo Dah - Louis Armstrong 1972
I Can See Clearly Now - Johnny Nash 1972
You Are So Beautiful - Joe Cocker 1974
Let 'Em In - Wings 1976
Old Time Rock & Roll - Bob Seger 1978
Smooth Operator - Sade 1985
I Want Your Love - Transvision Vamp 1988
Simply Irresistible - Robert Palmer 1988
The Power of Love - Celine Dion 1993
I Hope You Dance - Le Ann Womack 2000
Regresa a Mí (Unbreak My Heart) - Il Divo 2004
See You Again - Carrie Underwood 2013
I Still Talk to Jesus - Colin Stough 2023

1930s

Top right to left:
Memaw on the far left with her siblings and their significant others / Baby Wanda with the family dog / Bob's baby footprint / Wanda with her niece Connie / The Inmon family farmhouse built by Loyf Inmon / Young Bob with his younger sisters Margo and Denise / Grandpa Harsh the barber, Bob's grandpa / Grandma Browne (Madeline) with her son Bob / Carl Sell and son Bob / 3-year old Bob and chickens

1940s

Top right to left:
Wanda with her siblings (clockwise from top left) Marilyn, Weldon, Kenneth B., Wynona, Dorothy, and young Wanda / Young Wanda with her cousin Frankie/ Wanda on a horse / Uncle Bob and young Bob / Grandma Browne, Grandma Harsh (Bob's grandma), and Aunt Salty (Loiselta, Bob's Aunt/Uncle Bob's wife) / Uncle Bob, Grandma Browne, Carl Sell, and Bob / Carl Sell, Bob, Aunt Salty, and Uncle Bob / Wanda / Bob with his horse, Lucky

1950s

Top right to left:
Pawpaw, baby Angie, and Memaw / Angie and Wanda / Angie and Wanda on a horse / Wanda (second from left) with her friends / Bob and Wanda's wedding / Bob and young Angie with Wanda's family on the Inmon farm / Wanda graduating high school / Angie and Wanda / Wanda and her friend Joyce in Dallas / Bob playing cards with his dog / Bob and Wanda on their honeymoon in Big Bear Lake, California

1960s

Top right to left:
Bob and baby Alicia / Bob, Alicia, Wanda, and Angie / Bob and baby Alicia / Grandma Browne with Grandma Harsh, her mom / Bob fishing / Bob, Wanda, Grandma Browne (Madeline, Bob's mom) and Brownie (Bob's second stepdad) / Loyf and Leona aka Pawpaw and Memaw (Wanda's parents) with dogs / Uncle Bob and Alicia / Pawpaw, Memaw, Angie, Wanda, Alicia, and Bob with Bob Jr. on his shoulders / Wanda

1970s

Top right to left:
Bob Jr., Wanda, Grandma Browne, Bob, baby Cindy, and Alicia / Cindy, Alicia, Bob Jr., and Wanda at Niagara Falls / Wanda playing frisbee in Texas / Wanda and a cockatoo / Wanda, Alicia, and Cindy with puppy Princess / Wanda, Alicia, Bob Jr., and Cindy / Bob with his sister Denise on his lap (she is pregnant with Angie Lane) / Alicia, Bob Jr., Angie, Wanda, Cindy, and Bob / Wanda / Bob and Wanda / Cindy and Wanda at Disneyland / Alicia with kitten Felix

1980s

Top right to left:

Bob with Gareeb / Bob with Shogun (his pet Goose) / Wanda with horses and Zambucka / Bob with horse and Rolls Royce / Wanda, Grandma Browne, and Aunt Margo (Bob's sister) / Aunt Dot and Wanda (sisters) / Bob and Cindy at their backyard pool in Snohomish, Washington / Alicia singing on stage in her band / Wanda / Bob playing pool in the garage/ Zambucka, Jody, and Wanda / Bob laughing / Bob Jr., Wanda, and Grandma Browne / Baby Ashley and Angie's cat, Monkey / Wanda and Ashley / Bob with Marinka / Matt on Gareeb / Bob on Gareeb / Wanda on Gareeb

1990s

Top right to left:

Wanda and Bob in Hawaii / Bob with his sister Denise / Wanda at the annual La Conner, Washington, tulip festival / Jacobe, Wanda, and Tim / Bob goofing around in Grandma Browne's accessories / Bob, Wanda, and newborn Jacobe / Terrisa, Jacobe, Bob Jr., and Kaelin / Ashley, Cindy, and Sham on Christmas / Ashley, Bob Jr., Kaelin, Bob, Jacobe, and Alicia / Wanda, Bob, and Alicia in Hawaii / All of the grandkids: Matt, Kaelin, Jacobe, Ashley, and Tim / Bob with his mother, Grandma Browne, at her house in Oregon / Wanda, Kaelin, Terrisa, Jacobe, Grandma Browne, and Ashley / Ashley and Jacobe / Ashley, Cindy, Wanda, and Alicia in Seattle / Ashley and Cindy in Snohomish / Bob and Wanda

2000s

Top right to left:

Wanda, Karen (Bob's cousin), Bob, and Aunt Denise / Bob and Cindy dancing at Cindy's 40th birthday party / Blondie and Alicia / Bob and BayBe / Bob and Wanda holding hands at Ashley's film school graduation in Seattle / Ashley and Bob at Cindy's 40th birthday party / Bob and Wanda in Las Vegas / Bob at Ashley's high school graduation / Bob with Alicia playing the piano / Blondie and Ashley / Bob, Jacobe, and Wanda at Jacobe's homecoming celebration / Wanda and Bob Jr. / Bob and Cindy / Tim, Ashley, and Matt in California

2010s

Top right to left:
Angie and Wanda in Seattle / Marilyn and Wanda (sisters) in Texas / Wanda and Cindy in Seattle / Kaelin and Wanda / Alicia and BayBe / Angie and her newborn granddaughter, Raleigh / Wanda, Kaelin, and Bob / Wanda in the La Conner tulip fields / Jacobe, Kaelin, and Ashley at Kaelin's high shool graduation / Wanda with BayBe

2020s

Top right to left:
Wanda and Kaelin on Wanda's 90th birthday / Kim (Kaelin's mother-in-law), Kyle, and Kaelin at their weddding shower / Matt, Raleigh, and Shandi / Kaelin and Wanda at Kaelin's wedding dress fitting / Cindy, Bob Jr., Angie, and Alicia at the La Conner home before it was sold / Jacobe, Wanda, and Blondie on Wanda's 90th birthday / Wanda and Charlie / Cindy and Wanda at the Seattle arboretum / Noah, Ashley, and Darby

FORGET-ME-NOTS

Noah Rael,
my live, laugh, love. For co-piloting together. For co-parenting gremlins. For creating a safe and loving home where I can laugh and be weird. For being proud of me. For thinking it's cute when my shirt is on backwards and there are crumbs on it.

My Mom,
thank you for always rooting for me, for raising me, providing for me, loving me, giving me my peanut butter and chocolate addiction, and for buying me salami sandwiches during that period growing up when I was obsessed with salami (the way Edgar in the opening scene of *Men in Black* is obsessed with sugar). For being THE Suzi Homemaker. Also, you were right; I should have taken cooking classes as a teenager.

Nana and Pops,
"for being kind, decent, unfailingly generous people. They are my twin pillars, without whom I could not stand. I am proud to be their grandchild." (to quote Rory Gilmore from the Season 3 finale of *Gilmore Girls*) You've always fueled my dreams and continue to do so. I miss you.

Aunt Angie,
for telling me that Nana would be proud of me. For taking me to see The Cramps when it was definitely not your cup of tea.

Uncle Bob,
thank you for being a solid rock in my life and helping me buy my first car. I'm sorry I crashed it.

Aunt Cindy,
for always being there for me, taking me to Backstreet Boys concerts, and teaching me sick dance moves. "Whatever." IYKYK

Jacobe,
for being my ride or die.

Kaelin,
for your 11/10 sense of humor and being a role model to me.

And to all of my not-so-distant family members who helped make this book come true, including Angie Lane, Connie, Janet Kay, Jody, Karen, LeighAnne, Matt, and Shandi, Mike and Suwarni, Randy, Sham, and Terrisa.

My Zetter Rael fam,
for including me in countless nights of breaking bread and reminding me that life is to be enjoyed. For making me laugh. A toast to Carla for sharing her kitchen, baking knowledge (especially her pie crust recipe), and for giving me my first copy of the *Betty Crocker Cookbook*. Grace, for making the tile background for the food photography. David and Mark, for having handcrafted ceramics and cutting boards ripe for the picking. Linda, for boldly testing so many recipes alongside your grandkids.

Erika Seward,
my die, cry, hate. For reminding me always to see the beauty. For always always always believing in me.

Katherine Jardine,
for being the KatDog to my Smash. For telling me she can picture my stories as vividly as she pictures the stories of her favorite authors.

Holly Bailey,
for being the MVP of this cookbook project, for contributing so much of your time to recipe testing and editing. From one granddaughter to another grandmother, thank you.

Lee Voreis,
for fixing my grandma's sifter.

Lorraine Marchant,
for helping finish my grandma's family quilts.

Vanessa Salvia,
from the bottom of my heart, for editing this book and creating the index.

Abigail Agersea,
for saying YES to having your illustrations in this book. Including your art inspired me to make this more than just a family project.

Fayte Yang Michaluk, Freya Kargard, Herman Esau, and Jamie Letourneau,
for your graphic design guidance.

My Artifact work fam,
for being daily taste testers and unconditional supporters of this project.

Annalise Rice,
your Friday morning lessons on creating room vignettes helped me in the design of this book! "You're family"

Outlet PDX,
for giving me the tools and guidance to make something I felt was missing from the world.

Mary from Brown Printing,
for your professional printing candor and for helping me make this project come true.

Kara Elder,
for recommending Vanessa Salvia to be my book editor.

Andrea Morris,
for your willingness to partake in this project.

Bert Krages and The Author's Guild,
for legal counsel.

The Cookbook Love Podcast by Maggie Green, whose episodes provided constant inspiration while working on this cookbook.

Starflower PDX, Buy Now/Pay Later apps on floral delivery websites, the discount flower section at my local grocery store, and to my neighbors with overgrown yards: thanks for the flowers.

For proofreading drafts of this book for me, with me, and without me:
Alicia Sell, Angela Vaughn, Ari Owens, Carla Zetter Rael, Holly Bailey, Kaelin Sell, Katherine Jardine, Kinsey Miller, Erika Seward, and Melissa Haskin's Recipe Editing 101 students.

Every volunteer who test-drove a recipe in this book:
Abigail Agersea, Amanda Wozab, Amy Pombo, Angela Vaughn, Annalise Rice and family, Ann Occhi, Ari Owens, Arizona Guerrero, Brooke Llewellyn, Carla Zetter Rael, Carly Hardman, Carolin Palmer, Christy Fish, Cindy Sell, Connie Stuart, Cynthia Rocconella, Daryl S., Denise Hudson, Dolly Dunbar, Fayte Yang Michaluk, Gina Gray, Grace Rael, Heather Johnson, Holly Bailey, Holly Wheeler, Jenni Fennerl, Jill Ripes, Jill Traxler, Julianna Mitchell, Karen Fink, Katherine Jardine, Kathy Veenhuizen, Kimberly Makris, Kinsey Miller, Laura Treptow, Laurie Palmer, Linda Zetter, Lorraine Marchant, Maggie Parker, Noel Cummings, Patricia Brent, Paul Reinhertz, Regan Zetter, Russell Hodgkinson, Sally Niedermeyer, Sandra Mendive, Shandi Sisserson, So-Min Cotik, Summer S. Broeckx-Smith, Sydney Viengluang, Tiana Monk, Tina Rooney, and Valerie Jackson.

Every single person who donated their hard-earned doll hairs to make this book a reality:
Alicia Sell, Anastasia Baranova, Angie Lane, Angie Vaughn, Annie Murai, Bob Sell Jr., Carla Zetter Rael, Cheryl Webber, Christy Fish, Cindy Sell, Erika Seward, Erin Holcomb, Grace Rael, Hilary Spray, Jake Nielson, Jenn McPoland, Jody Vinson, Jordan Hamilton, Joy Shamburger, Kamala Saxton, Karen Prince, Katherine Jardine, Kathy Veenhuizen, Laura Treptow, Lorraine Marchant, Leah Meijer, Kimberly Madrigal, Linda Zetter, Matt and Shandi Sisserson, Melanie Gaston, Michael Sawyer, Morgan Hendrickson, Paul Palmer, Val Morgan, and Vanessa Phillips.

Thank you for inspiration in rediscovering some family favorite recipes:
Allrecipes.com:
Beef and Beer Stew, Beef Brisket, Chocolate-Covered Peanut Butter Rounds, Chocolate Sauce, Cowgirl Caviar, Frito Pie, Bread and Butter Pickles, Hot Chocolate, Steak Stroganoff, and White Chicken Chili
TastesBetterFromScratch.com:
Cherry Pie, German Chocolate Cake, and Candied Pecans
Haley Chin, HaleysComment.org:
Green Bean Casserole
Blair Lonergan, TheSeasonedMom.com:
Southern Fried Catfish
Amy Nash, HouseOfNashEats.com:
Southern Hush Puppies

Dorothy: But it wasn't a dream. It was a place! And you, and you, and you, and you were there! But you couldn't have been, could you?

Auntie Em: We dream lots of silly things...

Thank you, to all of you, for helping me make this silly dream come true.

Ashley with who she is pretty sure is the real Dorothy at her Wizard of Oz themed birthday party in preschool. Early 1990s.

Wanda’s box of recipes.

INDEX

F

Q

R

S

T

WHAT'S COOKING GOOD LOOKING

Based on the life and love of

WANDA THE WILD

A family story of Southern cooking.

With a pinch of Midwest winsome, a dash of Mid-Atlantic charm, and a spoonful of West Coast warmth.